Easy Quilts *By Jupiter!*®

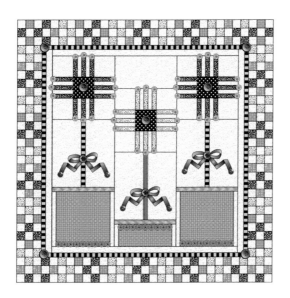

MARY BETH MAISON

That Patchwork Place®

Easy Quilts

Credits

Editor-in-Chief . . . . Barbara Weiland
Technical Editor . . . . Laura M. Reinstatler
Managing Editor . . . . Greg Sharp
Copy Editor . . . . Liz McGhee
Proofreader . . . . Tina Cook
Text and Cover Design . . . . Laura Jensen
Typesetting . . . . Laura Jensen, David Chrisman
Photography . . . . Brent Kane
Illustration and Graphics . . . . Brian Metz

Easy Quilts . . . By Jupiter!®
© 1994 by Mary Beth Maison
That Patchwork Place, Inc.,
PO Box 118, Bothell, WA 98041-0118 USA

Mission Statement

We are dedicated to providing quality products that encourage creativity and promote self-esteem in our customers and our employees. We strive to make a difference in the lives we touch.

That Patchwork Place is an employee-owned, financially secure company.

Printed in the United States of America
99 98 97 96 95 94   6 5 4 3 2 1

Library of Congress Cataloging-in-Publication Data
Maison, Mary Beth.
   Easy quilts—by Jupiter / Mary Beth Maison.
      p. cm.
   ISBN 1-56477-068-0 :
   1. Quilting—Patterns. 2. Appliqué—Patterns. 3. Quilts.
4. Flowers in art. 5. Heart in art. I. Jupiter (Firm) II. Title.
TT835.M2716 1994
746.9'7—dc20
                     94-17061
                     CIP

Dedication

For Gene, my husband, who makes everything possible.
   For my children, Jaclyn, Bo, and Brandon.
   —Yes, I'm coming home now.

Acknowledgments

A special thanks . . .

To Anna Leonard, for lending her optimism and talent.

To Karen and Ericka Boyd, for their ability to take over where I leave off!

To Linda Heinholdt, for appearing out of nowhere and machine quilting everything—so quickly too!

To Virginia Sutton Halonen, for being my friend and writing the "Biography"—not to mention countless other favors!

To Mimi Sell who embellished Red Hot Valentines.

A special thanks to my mother, Cam Martin, and my sister Ann for taking time out of their busy lives to type what seemed like endless pages.

Thanks to my friends in Q.A. Club—especially, Mary Dyer, Mary Andra Holmes, and Nancy Shamy—for their help in finishing bindings.

Thanks to the following fabric companies for creating the glorious, inspirational color selections I used in these projects.
    V.I.P. of Cranston Print Works
    Concord Fabrics, Inc.
    Peter Pan Fabrics, Inc.
    Fabri-Quilt by Virginia Robertson
    Hoffman-International Fabrics
    P & B Textiles
Finally, thanks to whoever invented the fax machine!

—Mary Beth Maison

Contents

Meet the Designer

ROCKY MCPHERSON

Mary Beth Maison is a newlywed and mother of six (three adopted and three stepchildren), as well as a designer, artist, quilter, and business owner. A lifelong Arizona resident, she lives in Phoenix with her new husband, Gene. Her artistic abilities seem to run in the family—her father is an architect, and her sisters are graphic designers.

Her interest in design began with quilting. What started as a hobby soon moved to employment in a quilt shop, where she studied fabrics and developed a fabric fading kit before branching off into designing her own patterns. These patterns are still available and have appeared in major publications, such as *McCall's, Country Quilting,* and *Creative Quilting.*

With the adoption of three children in 1986, she developed her own business so she could be home with her new family. By Jupiter!® has now expanded into a retail and mail-order business offering a line of original patterns, fabric fading kits, and a multitude of buttons and brass charms. She is particularly interested in embellishments, offering special classes in their use and in jewelry making.

Easy Quilts is Mary Beth's second book. Her first, *Victorian Charm,* was published by Taylor Made Designs.

introduction

When That Patchwork Place asked me to write this book, I was thrilled. Right away, I put together some new ideas, which inspired another idea, which led to another idea, and so on. Having a short attention span usually limits me to quick-and-easy projects. I try to keep all pieces simple and fun. Using bold new color combinations was part of the joy I had in creating these whimsical wall hangings.

The theme of hearts and flowers held a special meaning for me this year: While this book was in the works, I became engaged, then married, acquiring three stepchildren in addition to my three children! The partial manuscript survived as I moved my office out of my home while we renovated the house. Did I mention running a growing business full time?

Now that the dust has settled, I hope to move on to new inspirations and to living happily ever after.

Enjoy!

Tools and Supplies

Scissors

Use your best scissors to cut fabric only. To cut tiny appliqué pieces and thread, use scissors with short blades and sharp points that cut all the way to the ends. For cutting plastic templates, use paper-cutting scissors.

Thimbles

Thimbles are mostly a matter of personal preference, and there are many types to choose from, including ones with an opening for long fingernails. You may want to experiment. Most beginners (and pros!) like the brass-rimmed types for quilting. Some individuals use rubber thimbles, which help grip the needle. Plastic thimbles and traditional metal thimbles are sufficient.

The rimmed thimbles usually are best for beginners. If you can't find one, try a small piece of duct tape or surgical tape over the end of a plain metal or plastic thimble to help grip the needle and keep it from slipping.

Templates

Make your templates from see-through plastic, available at quilt shops or through mail order. Use plain white paper when you reverse templates for the fusible appliqué method. (See pages 8–9.)

Rotary Cutter and Mat

For those unfamiliar with rotary cutting, a brief introduction is provided here. For more detailed information, see Donna Thomas's *Shortcuts: A Concise Guide to Rotary Cutting* (That Patchwork Place).

1. Fold the fabric and match selvages, aligning the crosswise and lengthwise grains as much as possible. Place the folded edge closest to you on the cutting mat. To make a cut at a right angle to the fold, align a square ruler along the folded edge of the fabric. Then place a long, straight ruler to the left of the square ruler, just covering the uneven raw edges of the left side of the fabric.

Remove the square ruler and cut along the right edge of the long ruler, rolling the rotary cutter away from you. Discard this strip. (Reverse this procedure if you are left-handed.)

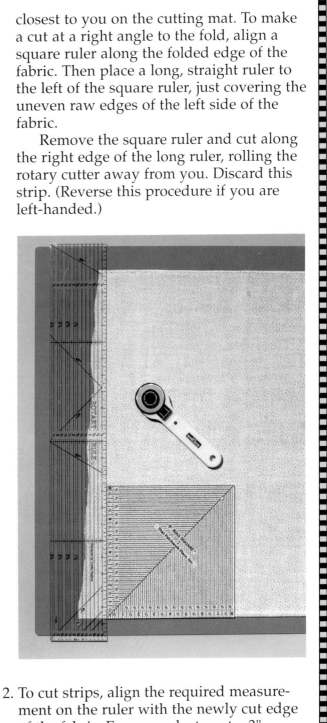

2. To cut strips, align the required measurement on the ruler with the newly cut edge of the fabric. For example, to cut a 3"-wide strip, place the ruler's 3" mark on the edge of the fabric, then cut

along the ruler's edge. All of the measurements for cut strips in this book include ¼"-wide seam allowances. Therefore, a 3"-wide cut strip, with a ¼"-wide seam allowance on each long edge, will finish to 2½" wide.

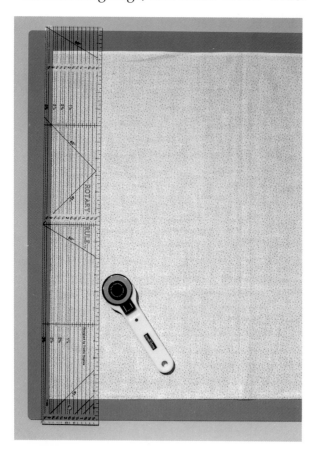

3. To cut squares, cut strips in the required widths. Trim away the selvage ends of the strip. Align the required measurement on the ruler with the left edge of the strip and cut a square. Continue cutting squares until you have the number of squares needed.

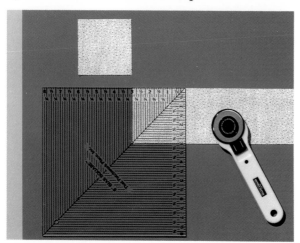

Marking Tools
A variety of tools are available to mark fabrics when tracing around templates or indicating quilting lines. Use a regular No. 2 pencil or fine-lead mechanical pencil for marking on paper, iron-on transfer paper, and light-colored fabrics. Use a silver or yellow marking pencil on darker fabrics. Chalk pencils or chalk-wheel markers also make clear marks on fabric. Be sure to test whatever tool you decide to use on your fabric to make sure the marks can be removed easily.

Fabrics and Colors

Always select high-quality, 100% cotton fabrics for your quilts. They hold their shape well and are easy to handle. Yardage requirements are provided for all of the projects in this book and are based on 42" inches of usable fabric after preshrinking. Some quilts call for ⅛-yard pieces or an assortment of scraps. If you have access to scraps, feel free to use them and purchase only those fabrics you need to complete the quilt you are making.

Preshrink all fabric to test for colorfastness and remove excess dye. Wash dark and light colors separately so that dark colors do not run or bleed onto light fabrics. Some fabrics may require several rinses to eliminate the excess dyes. Press fabrics so that you can cut out the pieces accurately.

Sometimes I like to use a zippy little striped print fabric for the borders and binding. If you want the same look but cannot find a stripe that works, try a contrasting dot print or the whimsical look of plaids. Checked prints add "busyness" and can be cut for an effect similar to stripes.

In this series of quilts, I used jewel tones—the wild Sunflowers quilt looks "van Gogh-ish" when made in bright colors. But all of these patterns can also be made in pastel colors to create a soft Victorian look.

Thread

Use good-quality, all-purpose 100% cotton or cotton-covered polyester thread.

For hand appliqué, match the color of the thread to the piece being appliquéd. If it is not possible to match the color exactly, choose thread that is slightly darker than the fabric. If the appliqué fabric contains many different colors, choose a neutral-colored thread that blends with the predominant color. (Directions for hand appliqué begin on page 8.)

For cheater appliqué, use quilting thread or one strand of embroidery floss in a contrasting color. If you use embroidery floss, use a short length (14"–16") and wax it to prevent knotting. (Directions for the cheater appliqué method begin on page 9.)

Buttons and Charms

A large selection of buttons and charms is helpful for embellishing these quilts. If your selection seems limited, try dyeing plain, white plastic buttons with Rit Dye, using the following procedure:
1. Fill a saucepan half full of water.
2. Add about ¼ package or container of Rit Dye (powder or liquid).
3. Heat to a simmer.
4. Put buttons in a sieve or strainer and dip into the dye. The color takes right away.
5. Rinse and dry buttons.

A great assortment of buttons by the pound and charms are available from By Jupiter!®. See "Resources" on page 75.

Batting and Backing

Choose a thin, polyester batting for these quilts. You can use cotton batting, but plan on quilting it closely—at least every 2"—to help it keep its shape. Cut batting at least 1" larger than the finished quilt top on all sides.

Backing can be any solid or printed fabric that is 100% cotton. Prewash the fabric to avoid shrinkage and color bleeding later. A print backing hides embellishing stitches, while a solid color backing shows off quilting stitches. Cut backings at least 2" larger than the finished quilt top all around.

General Instructions

These quilts require simple piecing and appliqué techniques. There are many different appliqué stitches and methods. You may use your choice of hand, "cheater," or fusible appliqué as explained on pages 8–9, or use your favorite method of machine appliqué.

Hand Appliqué

1. Lightly trace the shapes to be appliquéd onto the *right* side of the appliqué fabrics. Cut out these shapes, adding a ⅛"–¼" seam allowance all around.

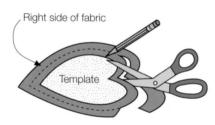

Right side of fabric

Template

2. Turn under the raw edges. Edges covered by other pieces need not be turned under or stitched down.

3. Position, pin, and appliqué the pieces in place, starting with the bottom layers and working up to the top layers. Use a blind stitch and an appliqué needle. For tips on thread, see page 7. Use the point of the needle or a round toothpick to turn under the raw edges. Turn under just enough to hide the marked lines on each piece.

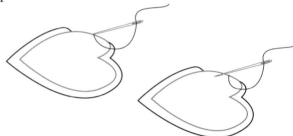

Clip inside curves and corners as you go, but only if necessary to make the edges smooth.

Fusible Appliqué

To fuse appliqués in place, you will need a fusible transfer web such as Pellon® Wonder-Under or HeatnBond.

1. In order to do the fusible method, *all designs must be reversed*. Using a dark pen or pencil, trace each design from the pattern page onto white paper. Flip the paper over and the traced design will show through. Trace along the design lines on the flip side. Cut out this paper pattern. The pattern is now reversed and ready to use for drawing templates.

Trace over line that shows through paper.

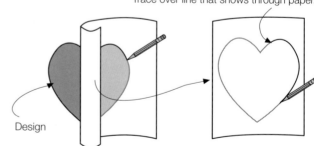

Design

2. Make durable templates from see-through plastic sheets, tracing around each paper pattern.

3. Draw around your templates on the fusible web's paper backing to make the fusible web pieces. Cut out at least ¼" away from the marked lines. Do not cut *on* the lines.

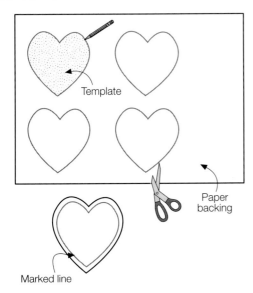

4. Place the fusible web pieces, paper backing side up, on the *wrong* side of the selected fabrics. Use a hot, dry iron to adhere the paper pieces to the fabric.

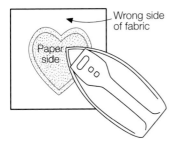

5. Let the fabric cool completely, then cut out all the shapes, cutting on the marked lines.

6. Peel the paper from the back of the cut shapes and position the appliqué on the background fabric. Referring to the manufacturer's instructions, fuse the appliqué pieces in place.

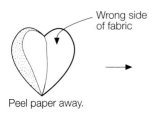

Cheater Appliqué

Cheater appliqué is quick and easy. You can cut your pieces in layers since there is no iron-on paper behind the fabrics and no line to follow as with hand appliqué. Cheater appliqué gives a textural quality that other appliqué methods do not. It looks best on solid fabrics or those with a subtle print.

For cheater appliqué, cut out each piece on the marked line; *do not add seam allowances or turn under the edges.* Using a contrasting quilting thread or one strand of embroidery floss, stitch to the background, using a running stitch ⅛" from the raw edges of each appliqué piece. To keep the embroidery floss from knotting, use a little wax on the floss.

Hand sew ⅛" from raw edge.

If your pieces require a lot of pins to hold them together, baste the pieces down, to avoid having the thread catch on the pins as you stitch around the outer edge of each piece.

To keep your background fabric flat, work on a tabletop rather than in your lap.

Machine Piecing

Machine piecing is the quickest way to sew patchwork pieces together. For hassle-free sewing, make sure your machine's tensions are set properly. Check your machine's manual for making adjustments.

Set the stitch length to 10–12 stitches per inch. There is no need to start and stop each line of stitching with backstitches.

Sew all seams with a consistent ¼"-wide seam allowance, unless otherwise noted, to ensure that all pieces and borders fit together accurately. Some machines have a special quilting foot designed so that the right and left edges of the foot measure exactly ¼" from the center needle position. If you do not have such a presser foot or cannot obtain one, take the time to establish an exact ¼"-wide seam guide on your machine.

1. Place a ruler or a piece of graph paper with four squares to the inch under your presser foot.
2. Gently lower the needle onto the first ¼" line from the right edge of the ruler or paper. Place several layers of tape, a piece of moleskin (available in drugstores), or a magnetic seam guide along the right-hand edge of the ruler or paper so it does not interfere with the feed dog. Test your new guide to make sure your seams are ¼" wide; if they are not, readjust your guide.

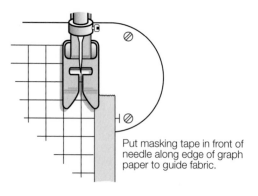

Put masking tape in front of needle along edge of graph paper to guide fabric.

Strong magnets can damage computerized machines, especially older models. If your machine is computerized, remove the magnetic seam guide when you finish sewing and store it away from the machine.

Chain Piecing

Chain piecing allows you to join many small pieces or units in a timesaving and efficient way.

1. Start by sewing the first pair of pieces. Sew from cut edge to cut edge, using 12–15 stitches per inch. At the end of the seam, stop sewing but do not cut the thread.

2. Feed the next pair of pieces under the presser foot, as close as possible to the first pair.
3. Keep feeding pieces through the machine without cutting the threads in between.

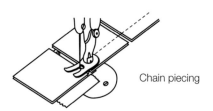

Chain piecing

4. When all the pieces have been sewn, remove the chain from the machine and clip the threads between the pieces.

Be consistent when you chain piece. Start with the same edge on each pair and the same color on top to avoid confusion. There is no need to backstitch since each seam will be crossed and held by another seam as the assembly process continues.

Hand Piecing

You may hand piece the patchwork in these quilts if you prefer. Simply make the templates ¼" smaller all the way around. (Subtract ½" from the overall dimensions given in the cutting directions.) For example, if a pattern requires a 3" x 6" rectangle, cut the template to measure 2½" x 5½" for hand piecing.

Cut the template from plastic template material. Trace around the template on the wrong side of the fabric to mark the stitching line. Mark a ¼"-wide seam allowance outside the seam line for the cutting line.

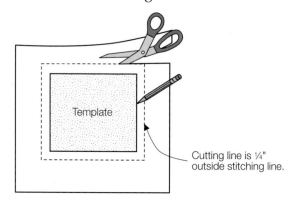

Template

Cutting line is ¼" outside stitching line.

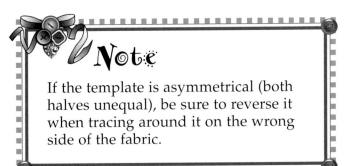

Note

If the template is asymmetrical (both halves unequal), be sure to reverse it when tracing around it on the wrong side of the fabric.

Follow the piecing diagrams given. Lay out your pieces into sections or rows. Place the first two pieces right sides together. Match and pin the beginning and ending of the sewing line. Accuracy is important for all corners and pieces to fit.

Thread a small needle with about 18" of matching thread. I use a quilting needle to make small hand stitches more easily.

Begin and end your stitching exactly on the beginning and ending of each seam line. Insert the needle and come up about ¹⁄₁₆" away from where you entered. Pull your thread through, leaving a small tail (¼") and backstitch to where you started. Take two backstitches in the same place to secure thread. Knots are unnecessary.

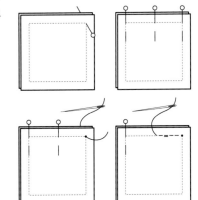

Continue with tiny running stitches. Constantly check the other side to make sure you are sewing on both marked seam lines. About every six stitches, take a tiny backstitch.

End your line of stitches with two backstitches. Clip the thread close to the fabric. Press seams as you go.

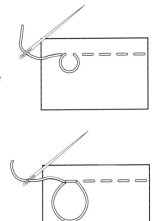

Pressing

Use a dry iron, as steam tends to distort the pieces. Press toward the darker fabric. Plan ahead so that the seam allowances will butt up against each other at seam intersections, reducing bulk and making it easier to join units.

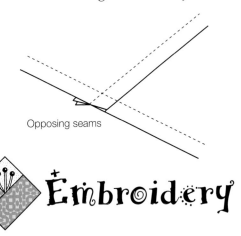

Opposing seams

Embroidery

Several of the quilt plans in this book include embroidered embellishments, requiring the stem stitch or the buttonhole stitch. Use two strands of embroidery floss for both.

Stem Stitch

The stem stitch is a good all-purpose stitch to use when a solid line is needed.

1. Bring the needle up through the fabric (A). Insert the needle at B, and bring it back out at C, about ⅛" away. Pull the thread through, keeping the thread below the needle.

2. Insert the needle at D, coming up again at B, where the needle went into the fabric for the last stitch. Pull the thread through, keeping the thread below the needle.

3. Continue, repeating steps 1 and 2, to create a smooth line.

Buttonhole Stitch

The buttonhole stitch can be used decoratively or functionally to hold down the edges of appliqué pieces.

1. To appliqué using the buttonhole stitch, begin by coming up from the back, right next to the edge of the appliqué piece. Insert the needle into the appliqué piece, about ¼" away from the edge and ¼" ahead of where the thread came out.

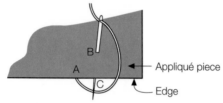

Appliqué piece

Edge

2. Bring the tip of the needle out next to the edge of the appliqué piece. Holding the thread under the needle, pull through just until snug. Be careful not to pull the stitches too tight or leave them too loose.

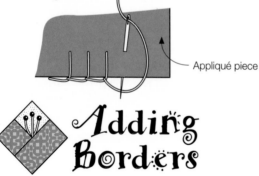

Appliqué piece

Adding Borders

Yardage requirements are calculated for cutting all borders across the width of the fabric from selvage to selvage.

For best results, do not cut border strips and sew them directly to the quilt sides without measuring first. The edges of a quilt often measure slightly longer than the distance through the quilt center, due to stretching during construction. Sometimes each edge is a different length. Cutting the border strips based on the dimensions of the outside edges results in a quilt with wavy borders. Instead, measure the quilt top *through the center* in both directions just before cutting each set of border strips to ensure that the finished quilt will be as straight and as "square" as possible.

Plain border strips are commonly cut along the crosswise grain and seamed where extra length is needed. Borders cut from the lengthwise grain of fabric require extra yardage, but seaming is then unnecessary.

1. Measure the width of the quilt top through the center. Cut border strips to that measurement, piecing as necessary. Mark the center of the quilt edges and the border strips. Pin the borders to the top and bottom of the quilt, matching the center marks and ends and easing as necessary. Sew the border strips in place. Press the seams toward the border.

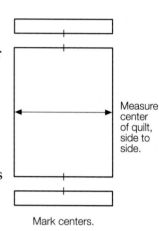

Measure center of quilt, side to side.

Mark centers.

2. Measure the quilt length through the center, including the top and bottom borders just added. Cut border strips to that measurement, piecing as necessary; mark the center of the quilt edges and the border strips. Pin the borders to the sides of the quilt top, matching the center marks and ends and easing as necessary. Sew the border strips in place. Press the seams toward the border.

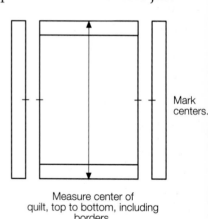

Mark centers.

Measure center of quilt, top to bottom, including borders.

Note

If you prefer, you may cut and sew borders to the sides first, then to the top and bottom edges.

Putting it All Together

1. Spread the backing, wrong side up, on a flat, clean surface. Anchor it with pins or masking tape. Be careful not to stretch the backing out of shape.
2. Spread the batting over the backing, smoothing out any wrinkles.
3. Place the pressed quilt top on top of the batting. Smooth out any wrinkles and make sure the edges of the quilt top are parallel to the edges of the backing.
4. Starting in the center, baste with needle and thread and work diagonally to each corner. Continue basting in a grid of horizontal and vertical lines 6"–8" apart. Finish by basting around the edges.

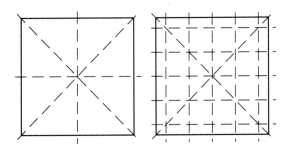

Quilting

Quilting may be done by hand or machine. To learn to do either method, it is best to see a demonstration. Local quilt shops are equipped with books and have teachers to help you. The quilting stitch is both a functional and decorative running stitch that holds the back, batting, and top together.

Hand Quilting

Hand quilting imparts a softer, more subtle line to the quilt. It is more time-consuming but well worth the effort. Strive for tiny, even stitches. First-timers should start with a No. 8 quilting needle and use quilting thread that is the same color as the fabric. Experienced quilters prefer a smaller needle.

Thread the needle and tie a small knot at one end of the thread. Put the needle through the *top* only and come up where you want to start quilting. Gently but firmly, tug on the thread to pop the knot through the top, hiding the knot in the batting.

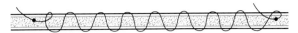

Starting the quilting thread

Wear a properly fitting thimble on your right middle finger. Start the stitch with the needle straight up and down, between your left index finger (underneath) and your right middle finger (on top). Reverse positions if you are left-handed.

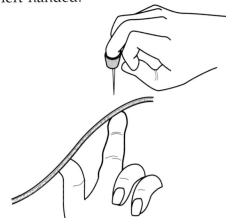

When you *barely* feel the tip of the needle underneath, tilt the needle all the way back against the fabric. Use only the thimble, not your fingers, to hold the position of the needle. You will need to do three things at the same time:

1. Tilt the needle back.
2. Push *up* with your left index finger, underneath, to make a *hill* at the point of the needle.
3. Place your right thumb in front of the needle and press down to make a valley.

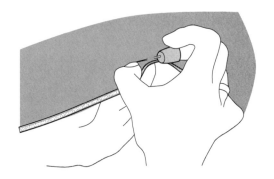

13

4. Once you have your hill and valley, *then* gently push the needle through. Only push through a tiny bit (a stitch length), then tilt the needle back into the fabric, straight up and down to repeat the hill and valley. Do three stitches at a time, then pull your thread through. *Practice, practice, practice!* Get used to the thimble; you can't do without it!

5. To finish off the thread, make a tiny knot close to the fabric and pop the knot under the fabric. Weave the needle through the batting, come up to the top, and clip the thread so no extra thread shows.

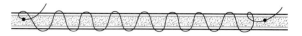

Ending the quilting thread

Most of the quilts in this book are embellished with buttons. If you wish to use a hoop to quilt, don't add the buttons until after the quilting is finished. The buttons interfere with the hoop's rings, making it difficult to achieve the proper tension.

Machine Quilting

Machine quilting gives a stronger line quality to the quilt and is much faster than hand quilting. If you prefer to machine quilt, use a walking foot on your machine. A standard foot applies pressure on the top layer of fabric, causing the three layers to shift. A walking foot lifts up in conjunction with each stitch, allowing all layers to move over the feed dog evenly. Check with your sewing machine dealer for a walking foot to fit your machine; your beautifully quilted results will be worth the initial cost.

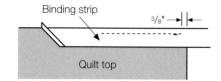

Walking foot attachment

Occasionally, instructions specify quilting in-the-ditch. That means quilting next to a seam, where there are no seam allowances lying under the quilt top, so that the stitches are almost hidden.

Basting for machine quilting is often done with safety pins; simply remove the pin just before quilting.

For a more professional look, pull quilting thread ends to the back, knot them, and work them into the quilt.

Binding

It is best to make a binding from 100% cotton fabric instead of using packaged bindings, which are usually a poly-cotton blend. These packaged bindings come in a limited range of colors and are less flexible than ones you make from 100% cotton. For straight edges, cut fabric strips across the fabric width.

1. Cut strips of fabric 1¼" wide. Sew them together at a 45° angle to make a strip long enough to go around all four sides, plus 3" for turning the corners.

Stitch on dotted line and trim seams to ⅛".

2. Press under one end of the binding strip at a 45° angle. Trim excess, leaving a ¼"-wide seam allowance as shown.

3. Trim the excess batting and backing even with the edges of the quilt top.

4. Place the binding strip along the side of the quilt top, right sides together and raw edges even. Using a ¼"-wide seam allowance, stitch the binding to the quilt top, stopping ⅜" from the raw edge at the corner. Backstitch. Remove from the machine.

Binding strip

⅜"

Quilt top

5. Fold the binding away from the edge of the quilt to form a 45° fold as shown. Refold the binding, making it even with the adjacent edge of the quilt. Stitch, beginning ⅜" from the corner and ending exactly ⅜" from the next corner. Repeat for the remaining edges of the quilt.

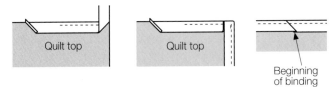

6. Turn the binding over to the back. Tuck under the raw edge and hand stitch the folded edge in place along the stitching. Do not stitch through to the front! At the corner, a folded miter will form on the front of the quilt. On the back, fold one side, then the other to create the miter. Stitch the miter to secure.

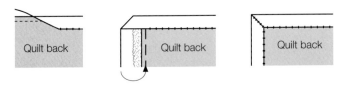

Adding Buttons and Charms

Add buttons and charms last, using six strands of embroidery floss. Choose different colors to make the look more interesting.

1. Thread the needle and knot the end. Enter through the top of the quilt where the button or charm will cover the knot. Go through to the back, take a tiny stitch, and return to the top of the quilt, coming up next to the knot.

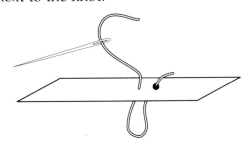

2. Thread the button and sew in place. Use only one or two stitches to secure. Hide the ending knot under the button. Only a couple of tiny, uniform stitches should show on the back of the quilt.

Charms can be clustered with buttons. Either hide the knots under the charms or leave tiny knots on the back.

Hanging Your Quilt

After all your efforts, your quilt deserves a place of honor. Find a cozy spot and brighten it with your latest creation. To display your quilt on the wall, take a few minutes to prepare it for hanging. Sew two or three cafe curtain rings or a hanging sleeve to the back of the quilt to allow you to hang the quilt without making pinholes in it.

Cafe Curtain Rings

On the back of the quilt, tack a ring to each end of the quilt at the top. Stitch only the lower edge of each ring so the upper edge can fit freely over a nail head. Make sure the rings won't be seen from the front when the quilt is hung, and take care not to stitch through to the front. If the quilt is wider than 18", attach a third ring to the center top as shown. To hang, loop the rings around pushpins or small nails in the wall.

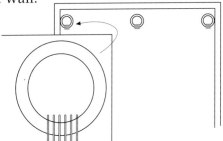

Hanging Sleeve

A hanging sleeve or rod pocket distributes weight evenly across the width of the quilt, allowing you to hang the quilt without stressing it.

1. Cut a strip of fabric 6"–8" wide and 1"–2" shorter than the finished width of the quilt at the top edge. Hem the ends. Fold the strip in half lengthwise, wrong sides together, and sew the long raw edges together with a ¼"-wide seam. Fold the tube so that the seam is centered on one side and press the seam open.

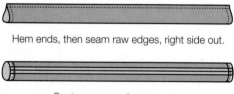

Hem ends, then seam raw edges, right side out.

Center seam and press open.

2. Place the tube on the back side of the quilt, just under the top binding, with the seamed side against the quilt. Hand sew the top edge of the sleeve to the quilt just below the binding, taking care not to sew through to the front of the quilt.

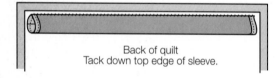

Back of quilt
Tack down top edge of sleeve.

3. Push the bottom edge of the tube up about ¼" and sew in place as shown. This will allow the hanging rod to slide through the tube into place without distorting or putting stress on the front of the quilt. Insert the hanging rod.

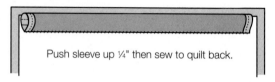

Push sleeve up ¼" then sew to quilt back.

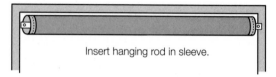

Insert hanging rod in sleeve.

4. Suspend the hanging rod on brackets, or attach screw eyes or drill holes at each end of the rod and slip the holes or eyes over small nails.

A LITTLE BIT OF FANCY by Mary Beth Maison, 1993, Phoenix, Arizona, 11" x 11". Plaids and stripes make this single layered heart fun and fancy. Embellished with a bow and buttons, it becomes a quick and easy way to send a message of love.

TREASURE HEARTS by Mary Beth Maison, 1993, Phoenix, Arizona, 17" x 23". A single border of checks and buttons surround three layered hearts, embellished with ribbon, brass charms, and special buttons. Make the quilt a personal statement by adding old jewelry or other treasures dear to the heart.

17

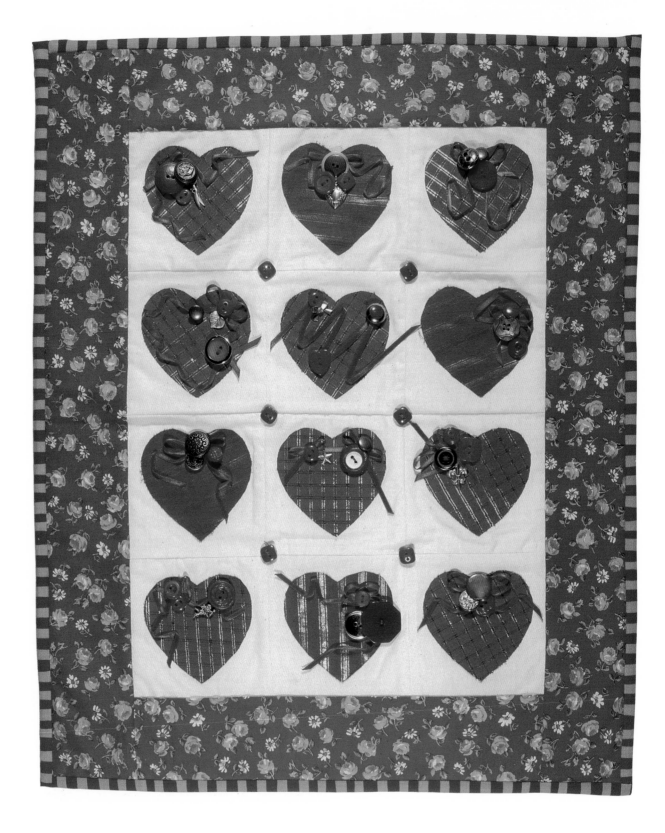

RED HOT VALENTINES by Mary Beth Maison, 1993, Phoenix, Arizona, 16" x 19½". Opposites do attract! Use a floral print for the border and a plaid for the hearts, then add romance with ribbons, buttons, and brass charms.

MY PURPLE HEARTS SING THE BLUES by Mary Beth Maison, 1993, Phoenix, Arizona, 11¼" x 18¼". Brass music charms and coordinating ribbons on somber purple and blue hearts make this piece sing from the heart and soul.

PANSY by Mary Beth Maison, 1993, Phoenix, Arizona, 11" x 18½". Having a delicate look, yet rich with color, this simple quilt makes a sweet gift or accent piece for decorating.

HEARTS AND PANSIES by Mary Beth Maison, 1993, Phoenix, Arizona, 18" x 32½". Hearts and pansies go together. A cheerful checked border surrounds these hearts and pansies in a charming quilt that begs for ribbon and button embellishments.

WILD SUNFLOWERS by Mary Beth Maison, 1993, Phoenix, Arizona, 18¾" x 35½". Bring sunflowers into your home year 'round. The zippy striped inner border makes these sunflowers into funflowers! Cheater appliqué in rich, warm colors on a cool blue background combined with random buttons add to the free and easy feeling.

SINGLE SUNFLOWER by Mary Beth Maison, 1993, Phoenix, Arizona, 17" x 17".
Vibrant colors and large overlapping leaves represent a wild sunflower, which overlaps
a spicy striped border. This quilt was made in memory of Mildred Fernyhough,
a wonderful neighbor who tended the wild flowers in our alley.

BASIC BOTANIA by Mary Beth Maison, 1993, Phoenix, Arizona, 17" x 23".
Stylized white flowers with embellished centers against a red background and
checkerboard border make this a zippy piece, great for Christmas or springtime.

PURPLE PASSION BOTANIA by Mary Beth Maison, 1993, Phoenix,
Arizona, 23½" x 23½". Purple is the perfect color for these flowers, with
buttons and tiny brass bee charms gracing each flower center. Green ribbon
and white lace are added for a romantic look.

POTTED WHIMSY by Mary Beth Maison, 1993, Phoenix, Arizona, 31" x 31".
Whimsical childlike flowers, surrounded by a happy checkerboard border and
embellished with buttons and charms, create sparkle for any corner of the home.
Add ribbon bows for leaves, and it's summer all year. Gardening has never been so easy!

ONE WHIMSY by Mary Beth Maison, 1993, Phoenix, Arizona, 29½" x 14¾". Whip up a single "Whimsy" in a day! Add ribbon for leaves and buttons for fun.

POTTED HEARTSIES by Mary Beth Maison, 1993, Phoenix, Arizona, 21" x 25½". Love blossoms in garden pots! Fanciful heart-shaped flowers and star-shaped "buds" dance across this fun quilt embellished with ribbons, buttons, and bows. Simple embroidery and small beads lend a "botanically correct" element to the "Heartsies."

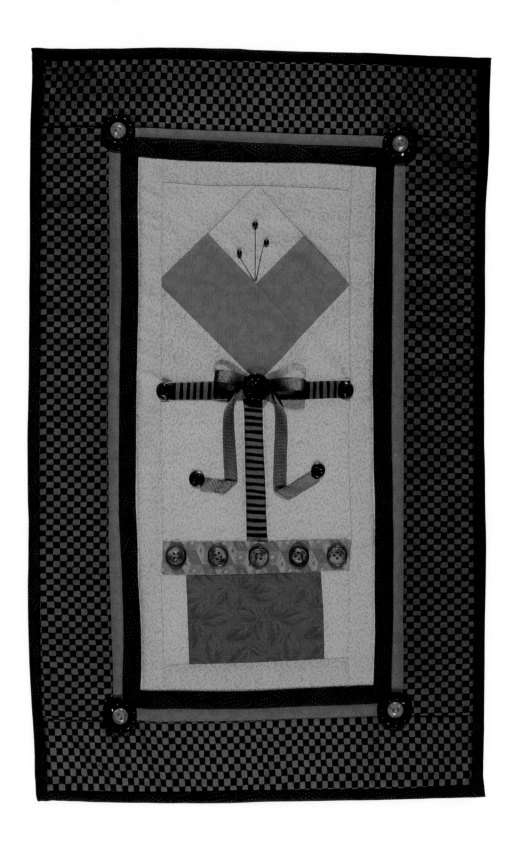

SINGLE HEARTSY by Mary Beth Maison, 1993, Phoenix, Arizona, 16" x 25".
As easy as can be, stitch up this touch of spring for the one you love.
Embellish with buttons, beads, simple embroidery, and a ribbon bow for a quick gift.

A Little Bit of Fancy

Finished Size: 11" x 11"
Color Photo: Page 17
Templates: Page 31

MATERIALS	CUTTING
⅜ yd. green print for background	1 square, 9" x 9"
¼ yd. red plaid for heart	1 large heart*
⅛ yd. gold print for heart	1 small heart*
⅛ yd. purple print for border	2 strips, each 1½" x 42"
⅛ yd. striped print for binding	2 strips, each 1¼" x 42"
⅓ yd. fabric for backing	1 square, 13" x 13"
13" x 13" square of batting	
12"-long piece of ⅝"-wide green ribbon	
5 buttons in assorted sizes and colors	
Embroidery floss in assorted colors	

* Cut hearts, using the templates on page 31, as directed for the appliqué method you prefer. (See the appliqué sections in "General Instructions" on pages 8–9.) The quilt in the photo was appliquéd using the fusible method.

29

Directions

1. Appliqué or fuse the large red heart to the center of the 9" green background square. Appliqué or fuse the small gold heart to the center of the red heart.

2. Following the instructions on page 12 for measuring and adding borders, cut and sew the side border strips to the quilt top, then add the top and bottom border strips as shown. Press the seam allowances away from the quilt center.

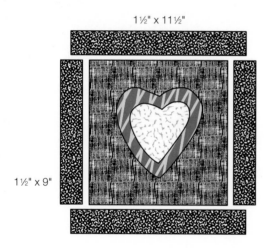

1½" x 11½"

1½" x 9"

3. If desired, add decorative stitches to embellish the hearts. (See pages 11–12.)

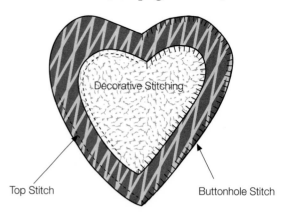

Decorative Stitching

Top Stitch

Buttonhole Stitch

4. Layer the completed quilt top with batting and backing; baste.
5. Hand or machine quilt.
6. Bind the edges.
7. Embellish with a folded ribbon and fancy buttons. Use different colors of embroidery floss to attach the buttons.

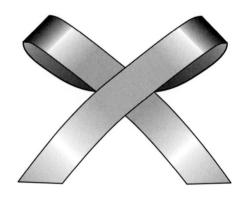

8. Add a hanging sleeve. (See page 16.)

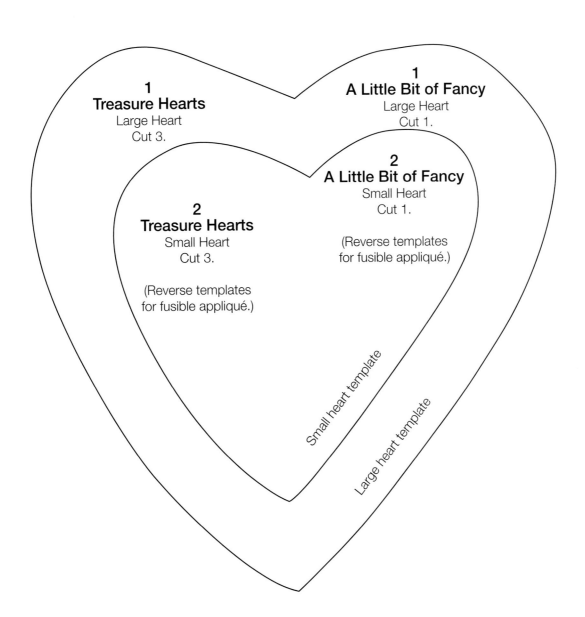

1
Treasure Hearts
Large Heart
Cut 3.

1
A Little Bit of Fancy
Large Heart
Cut 1.

2
A Little Bit of Fancy
Small Heart
Cut 1.

(Reverse templates
for fusible appliqué.)

2
Treasure Hearts
Small Heart
Cut 3.

(Reverse templates
for fusible appliqué.)

Small heart template

Large heart template

Treasure Hearts

Finished Size: 17" x 34"
Color Photo: Page 17
Templates: Page 31

MATERIALS	CUTTING
½ yd. green print for background and borders	2 squares, each 9" x 9"
	2 strips, each 1½" x 42"
⅝ yd. purple print for background and borders	1 square, 9" x 9"
	2 strips, each 1½" x 42"
	3 strips, each 2½" x 42"
7" x 7" square *each* of 3 gold prints	1 large heart from each fabric*
¼ yd. gold print for borders and binding	2 strips, each ¾" x 42"
	5 strips, each 1¼" x 42"

MATERIALS	CUTTING
5" x 5" square of black print (or use scraps)	1 heart center*
2 squares, each 5" x 5", of brown print (or use scraps)	2 heart centers*
⅔ yd. fabric for backing	
19" x 35" rectangle of batting	
1 yd. of ⅜"-wide black ribbon	
42 small black buttons in assorted shapes for hearts and pieced border	
8 small purple, yellow, and green buttons in assorted shapes for hearts	
Assorted charms (optional)	
1 skein gold embroidery floss	

* Cut hearts, using the templates on page 31, as directed for the appliqué method you prefer. (See the appliqué sections in "General Instructions" on pages 8–9.) The quilt in the photo was appliquéd using the fusible method.

Directions

1. Appliqué or fuse a black or brown heart to the center of each gold heart as shown.

2. Center the gold heart with black center onto the 9" purple square. Center each remaining gold heart on a 9" green square. Appliqué or fuse. Outline each gold heart with buttonhole stitches, using a double strand of gold embroidery floss. (See page 12 for buttonhole-stitch directions.)

3. Sew a green background block to the top and bottom of the purple background block as shown. Press the seam allowances in one direction.

+

+

4. Following the instructions on page 12 for measuring and adding borders, cut the ¾"-wide gold top and bottom border strips and sew them to the quilt top, then add the side border strips as shown. Press the seam allowances away from the quilt.

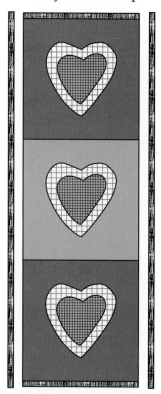

Note

Be sure to sew accurate ¼"-wide seams. The strip-pieced unit should measure 4½" wide, with each inner strip measuring exactly 1".

6. Cut at 1½" intervals across the strip-pieced unit to make 1½" x 4½" rectangles.

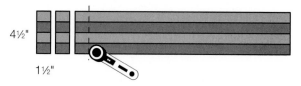

7. Join strip-pieced rectangles, alternating colors and removing squares as necessary to make top and bottom border strips of 9 squares each. Press the seam allowances in one direction.

Note

With a ¼"-wide finished border, use a scant ¼"-wide seam allowance to keep the seam allowances from running into each other and help the quilt lie flat.

Note

Measure the pieced border strips. If the measurement is different than the measurement of the quilt top, resew a few of the squares, taking a *slightly* deeper or shallower seam allowance until the border is the right length.

5. Sew the 1½" x 42" green and purple strips together to make a strip-pieced unit, alternating colors as shown. Press seam allowances in one direction.

8. Measure and adjust top and bottom border strips if necessary, then add to the quilt top. Press seam allowances away from the quilt center.

9. Join remaining strip-pieced rectangles, alternating colors and removing squares as necessary to make side border strips of 28 squares each. Press the seam allowances in one direction.

10. Measure and adjust the side border strips if necessary, then add to the quilt top. Press seam allowances away from the quilt center.

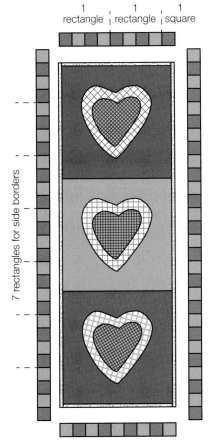

11. Measure and cut the 1¼"-wide gold border strips and sew them to the top and bottom of the quilt top; repeat for the side border strips. Press seam allowances away from the quilt center. (Refer to "Adding Borders" on page 12.)

12. Measure and cut the 2½"-wide purple border strips and sew them to the top and bottom of the quilt top; repeat for the side border strips.

13. Layer the completed quilt top with batting and backing; baste.

14. Hand or machine quilt in-the-ditch or use a quilt pattern of your choice.

15. Bind the edges.

16. Embroider a row of buttonhole stitching around the edge of each gold heart, using 2 strands of gold embroidery floss.

17. Add buttons, charms, and black ribbon bows as desired. Refer to the diagram below for placement ideas. Sew a black button to each purple square in the pieced border.

18. Add a hanging sleeve. (See page 16.)

Red Hot Valentines

Finished Size: 16¼" x 20"
Color Photo: Page 18
Template: Page 37

MATERIALS	CUTTING
⅓ yd. muslin for background	12 squares, each 4¼" x 4¼"
⅛ yd. red plaid for hearts*	12 hearts**
¼ yd. red print for border	2 strips, each 2¾" x 42"
⅛ yd. striped print for binding	2 strips, each 1¼" x 42"
½ yd. fabric for backing	
18" x 22" rectangle of batting	
3 yds. of ⅛"-wide red ribbon	
42 red and brass buttons in assorted small sizes	
6 brass charms (optional)	

* Use one plaid or different plaids of the same color.

** Cut hearts, using the template on page 37, as directed for the appliqué method you prefer. (See the appliqué sections in "General Instructions" on pages 8–9.) The quilt in the photo was appliquéd using the fusible method.

Directions

1. Appliqué or fuse each heart to the center of a 4¼" x 4¼" square of muslin.

2. If you wish, outline hearts now with a buttonhole stitch before embellishing. (See page 12.)

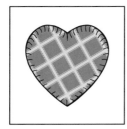

3. Arrange and sew blocks in rows; press seam allowances in opposite directions from row to row.

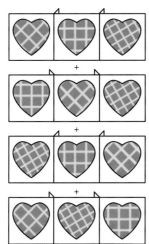

4. Sew rows together. Press.
5. Following the instructions on page 12 for measuring and adding borders, cut the 2¾"- wide top and bottom border strips and sew them to the quilt top; then add the side border strips. Press the seam allowances away from the quilt.

6. Referring to the quilt plan on page 36, add ⅛"-wide ribbon bows, positioning each ribbon differently for each heart. Tack the twists to the background with tiny hidden stitches; use matching thread or floss.
7. Sew the buttons and brass charms to each heart, choosing 3 to 5 buttons for each heart and varying the sizes and shapes. Refer to the quilt plan on page 36 for placement.
8. Layer the completed quilt top with batting and backing; baste.
9. Hand or machine quilt, tie with embroidery floss, or sew on buttons. The quilt in the photo on page 18 is tied with buttons secured to the block intersections with quilting thread.
10. Bind the edges.
11. Add a hanging sleeve. (See page 16.)

1
Red Hot Valentines
Cut 12.

My Purple Hearts Sing the Blues

Finished Size: 15" x 18½"
Color Photo: Page 19
Template: Page 39

MATERIALS	CUTTING
⅓ yd. gold solid or print for background and border	1 rectangle, 8½" x 12"
	2 strips, each 1" x 42"
¼ yd. purple print for hearts and border	3 hearts*
	2 strips, each 2¼" x 42"
⅛ yd. blue print for hearts (or use scraps)	3 hearts*
¼ yd. black print for border and binding	2 strips, each 1½" x 42"
	2 strips, each 1¼" x 42"
½ yd. backing fabric	
17" x 20" rectangle of batting	
½ yd. *each* of coordinating ¼"-wide blue and purple ribbon	
½ yd. of ¾"-wide black grosgrain ribbon	
12 assorted small yellow, blue, and purple buttons	
Assorted brass musical charms (optional)	
1 skein black embroidery floss	

*Cut hearts, using the template on page 39, as directed for the appliqué method you prefer. (See the appliqué sections in "General Instructions" on pages 8–9.) The quilt in the photo was appliquéd using the fusible method.

Directions

1. Following the instructions on page 12 for measuring and adding borders, cut the 1½"-wide black border strips and sew them to the top and bottom of the 8½" x 12" gold rectangle; repeat for the side border strips. Press seam allowances away from the quilt center.

2. Measure and cut the 1"-wide gold border strips and sew them to the top and bottom of the rectangle; repeat for the side border strips.

3. Measure and cut the 2¼"-wide purple border strips and sew them to the top and bottom of the rectangle; repeat for the side border strips.

4. Position 3 purple hearts and 3 blue hearts on the gold rectangle. For hand appliqué, remember to allow for the ¼"-wide seam allowances. Alternate the heart colors as shown in the color photo on page 19. Appliqué or fuse in place.

5. Add decorative stitches to the hearts as desired. Use 2 strands of black embroidery floss if you wish to buttonhole stitch the edges of the hearts. (See page 12 for button-hole-stitch directions.)

6. Layer the completed quilt top with batting and backing; baste.

7. Hand or machine quilt in-the-ditch or use a quilt pattern of your choice.

8. Bind the edges.

9. Embellish each blue heart with a purple bow and each purple heart with a blue bow. Add 2 buttons to each heart, and a brass charm if desired. Refer to the diagram for placement.

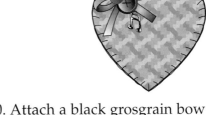

10. Attach a black grosgrain bow to the gold border in the upper left corner. Twist and tack the ends of the ribbon, using tiny stitches.

11. Add 2 buttons and optional brass charms to the bow as shown in the diagram.

12. Add a hanging sleeve. (See page 16.)

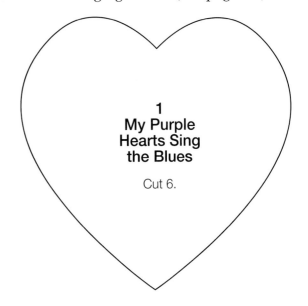

1
My Purple
Hearts Sing
the Blues

Cut 6.

Pansy

Finished Size: 11" x 18½"
Color Photo: Page 20
Templates: Page 42

MATERIALS	CUTTING
¼ yd. muslin for background	3 squares, each 4½" x 4½"
¼ yd. purple print for border and binding	2 strips, each 1" x 42"
	2 strips, each 1¼" x 42"
¼ yd. pansy print for border	2 strips, each 3¼" x 42"
⅛ yd. gold print or solid for petals (or use scraps)	3 Pansy Petal Template 4*
	6 Pansy Petal Template 5*
⅛ yd. dark purple print or solid for petals (or use scraps)	2 Pansy Petal Template 1*
	2 Pansy Petal Template 2*
	2 Pansy Petal Template 3*

MATERIALS	CUTTING
⅛ yd. fuchsia print or solid for petals (or use scraps)	1 Pansy Petal Template 1*
	1 Pansy Petal Template 2*
	4 Pansy Petal Template 3*
⅜ yd. fabric for backing	
13" x 21" rectangle of batting	
13 assorted small purple, fuchsia, and wood buttons	
4 brass leaf charms (optional)	
1 skein each of gold, purple, and fuchsia embroidery floss	

* Cut petals, using the templates on page 42, as directed for the appliqué method you prefer. (See the appliqué sections in "General Instructions" on pages 8–9.) The quilt in the photo was appliquéd using the fusible method.

Directions

1. Arrange and appliqué flower petals to each muslin square in numerical order, referring to the diagram for placement. If you use the fusible method, position and then fuse all the flower pieces at the same time.

2. Embellish the flowers as desired. Using 2 strands of floss, embroider 3 radiating lines from each petal's center as shown, using one long stitch for each line or a stem stitch. (See pages 11–12.)

3. Sew the blocks together in a vertical row as shown. Press.

4. Following the instructions on page 12 for measuring and adding borders, cut the 1"-wide purple print top and bottom border strips and sew them to the quilt top, then add the side border strips. Press seam allowances away from the quilt center.

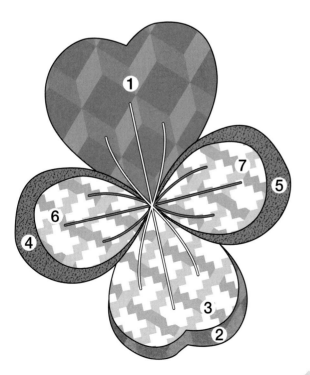

5. Measure and cut the 3¼"-wide pansy print border strips and sew them to the top and bottom of the quilt top; repeat for the side border strips.
6. Hand or machine quilt in-the-ditch or use your own pattern.
7. Bind the edges.
8. Sew 3 assorted colored buttons to each flower's center as shown in the diagram on page 15. Add a button and, if desired, a leaf charm to each corner of the purple inner border.
9. Add a hanging sleeve. (See page 16.)

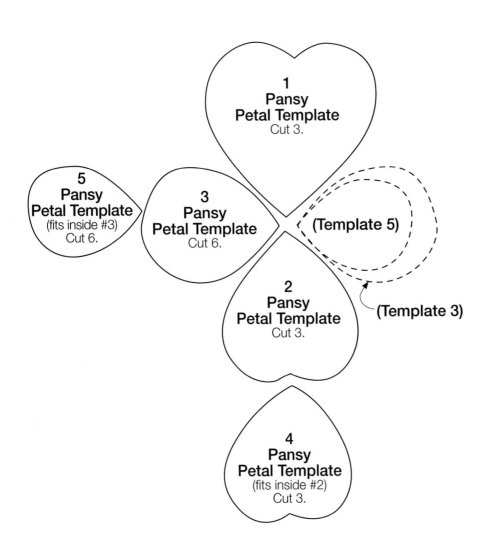

1
Pansy
Petal Template
Cut 3.

5
Pansy
Petal Template
(fits inside #3)
Cut 6.

3
Pansy
Petal Template
Cut 6.

(Template 5)

(Template 3)

2
Pansy
Petal Template
Cut 3.

4
Pansy
Petal Template
(fits inside #2)
Cut 3.

Hearts and Pansies

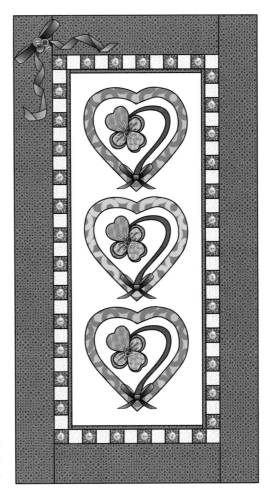

Finished Size: 18" x 33"
Color Photo: Page 20
Templates: Pages 42 and 47

MATERIALS	CUTTING
¼ yd. muslin for heart centers	3 small hearts (Hearts and Pansies Template 2*)
½ yd. purple print for hearts, pieced border, and binding	2 large hearts (Hearts and Pansies Template 1*)
	2 strips, each 1½" x 42"
	3 strips, each 1¼" x 42"
⅓ yd. purple print for middle heart (or use scraps)	1 large heart (Hearts and Pansies Template 1*)
¼ yd. dark green print or solid (or use scraps)	3 stems
½ yd. gold print or solid for background, pieced border, and flowers	1 rectangle, 10" x 25"
	2 strips, each 1½" x 42"
	3 Pansy Petal Template 4*
	6 Pansy Petal Template 5*

Continued on page 44.

Continued from page 43.

MATERIALS	CUTTING
⅛ yd. dark purple print for flowers (or use scraps)	3 Pansy Petal Template 1*
	3 Pansy Petal Template 2*
⅛ yd. fuchsia for flowers (or use scraps)	6 Pansy Petal Template 3*
½ yd. green print for inner and outer borders	2 strips, each ¾" x 42"
	3 strips, each 3¼" x 42"
⅝ yd. fabric for backing	
20" x 35" rectangle of batting	
1 yd. of ¼"-wide green ribbon	
½ yd. of ⅝"-wide dark purple grosgrain ribbon	
38 small gold or yellow buttons for hearts and corners	
9 assorted gold, green, purple, and fuchsia buttons	
2 brass charms for corner bow (optional)	
1 skein each of gold and fuchsia embroidery floss	

*Cut hearts and petals as directed for the appliqué method you prefer. (See the appliqué sections in "General Instructions" on pages 8–9.) Use pansy templates for the Pansy quilt, page 42; and use the heart and stem templates on page 47. The quilt in the photo was appliquéd using the fusible method.

Directions

1. Appliqué or fuse a muslin heart to the center of each large purple heart.

2. Appliqué or fuse a stem to each muslin heart. Refer to the template on page 47 for stem placement.

3. To each muslin heart, appliqué or fuse pansy petals in numerical order, covering stem end. See page 47 for petal placement.

Note

If you use the fusible-appliqué method, position all of the pansy petals on each heart and fuse at one time.

4. Using 2 strands of embroidery floss, embroider 3 gold lines from the pansy center on each purple heart petal, and 3 fuchsia lines on each gold petal.

5. Using 2 strands of embroidery floss, stitch a row of gold running stitches ⅛" inside the dark purple heart petal, and a row of fuchsia running stitches ⅛" inside each gold petal. See diagram above.

6. Fold the 10" x 25" gold background rectangle in half lengthwise, then crosswise, pressing lightly after each fold. Position the center heart, then position the top and bottom hearts 1¼" away from the top and bottom edges of the background rectangle. Appliqué or fuse the 3 hearts in place.

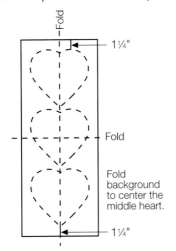

Fold

1¼"

Fold

Fold background to center the middle heart.

1¼"

BORDERS

1. Following the instructions on page 12 for measuring and adding borders, cut the ¾"-wide green top and bottom border strips and sew them to the quilt top, then add the side border strips. Press seam allowances away from the quilt center.

> ## Note
> For a ¼"-wide finished border, use a scant ¼"-wide seam allowance to keep the seam allowances from running into each other so the quilt will lie flat.

2. Sew the 1½" x 42" gold and purple border strips together to make a strip-pieced unit, alternating colors as shown. Press seam allowances in one direction.

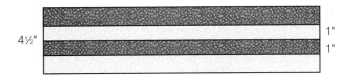

4½"

1"

1"

> ## Note
> Be sure to sew accurate ¼"-wide seams. The strip-pieced unit should measure 4½" wide, with each inner strip's width exactly 1".

3. Cut across the strip-pieced unit at 1½" intervals to make 1½" x 4½" pieced rectangles as shown.

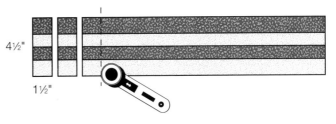

4½"

1½"

4. Join strip-pieced rectangles, alternating colors and removing squares as necessary, to make top and bottom strips of 10 squares each. Press the seam allowances in one direction.

HEARTS AND PANSIES

Note

Measure the pieced border strips. If the measurement is different than the measurement of the quilt top, resew a few of the squares, taking a *slightly* deeper or shallower seam allowance until the border is the right length.

5. Sew top and bottom pieced border strips to the quilt. Press seam allowances away from the quilt.
6. Join remaining rectangles, alternating colors and removing squares as necessary to make side border strips of 27 squares each. Press seam allowances in one direction.
7. Measure and, if necessary, adjust, then sew the side border strips to the quilt top. Press seam allowances away from the quilt center.

```
          1            1           2
       rectangle   rectangle   squares
```

3 squares

6 rectangles

8. Following the instructions on page 12 for measuring and adding borders, cut the 3¼"-wide green top and bottom border strips and sew them to the quilt top, then add the side border strips. Press seam allowances away from the quilt center.

FINISHING TOUCHES

1. Layer the completed quilt top with batting and backing; baste.
2. Hand or machine quilt in-the-ditch or use a quilt pattern of your choice.
3. Bind the edges.
4. Sew 1 yellow, 1 green, and 1 fuchsia or purple button to the center of each pansy. Sew a yellow button to each purple square in the pieced border.
5. Cut the ¼"-wide green ribbon into 3 equal lengths. Tie each ribbon into a bow and tack with tiny stitches to the base of each stem.

6. Attach a purple grosgrain bow to the outer green border in the upper left corner. Twist and tack the ends of the ribbon, using tiny stitches. Add 3 buttons and, if desired, brass charms to the bow.

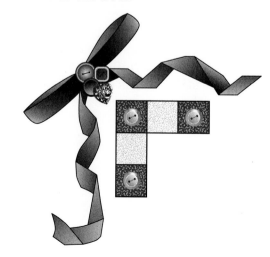

7. Add a hanging sleeve. (See page 16.)

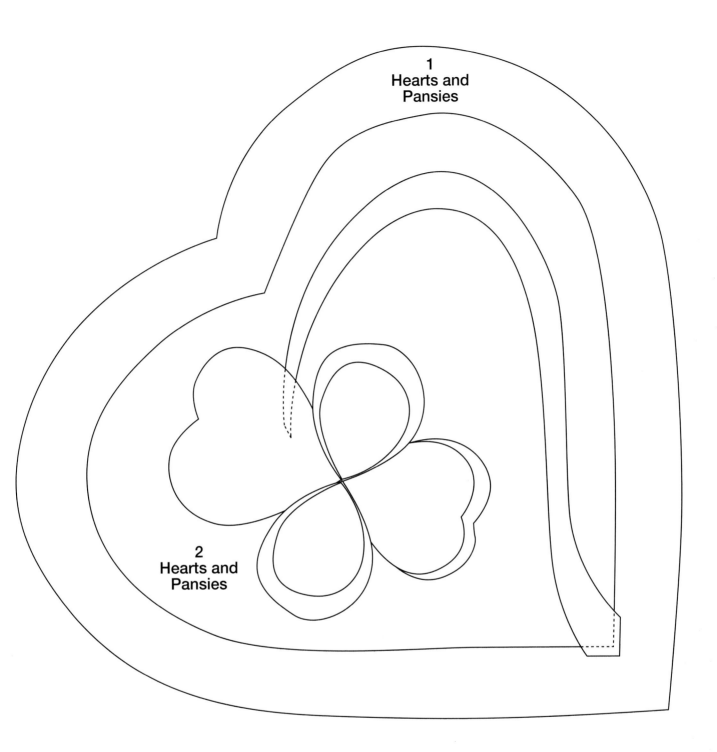

1
Hearts and
Pansies

2
Hearts and
Pansies

Remember to reverse templates for the fusible method.

Wild Sunflowers

Finished Size: 19" x 36½"
Color Photo: Page 21
Templates: Pages 52–53

The sunflowers in this quilt are unique in the randomness of their leaf and petal placement. When referring to the diagram for positioning leaves, petals, and centers, keep this randomness in mind, letting your creativity guide you.

For a more varied appearance, cut the petals using both sides of the template or cut some petals freehand. Speed up the cutting process by cutting fabric in layers.

Refer to the cutting chart for the number of each color's petals to use per sunflower.

MATERIALS	CUTTING
¾ yd. blue print or solid for background and border	1 rectangle, 11½" x 29"
	3 strips, 3½" x 42"
¼ yd. striped print for inner border and binding	5 strips, 1¼" x 42"
⅓ yd. green solid or print	2 leaves* (Leaf Template 1**)
	3 leaves* (Leaf Template 2**)
	3 leaves* (Leaf Template 3**)
¼ yd. *each* of 3 black prints (or use scraps)	3 flower centers* (1 *each* from Center Templates 1, 2, and 3)
⅛ yd. dark orange print (or use scraps)	21 petals* (7 *each* from Petal Templates 4, 5, and 6) Use 7 petals per sunflower.
⅛ yd. dark gold print (or use scraps)	18 petals* (6 *each* from Petal Templates 4, 5, and 6) Use 6 petals per sunflower.
⅛ yd. medium gold solid (or use scraps)	39 petals* (13 *each* from Petal Templates 7 and 8) Use 13 petals per sunflower.
⅛ yd. *each* light yellow print and solid (or use scraps)	18 petals of *each* color* (6 *each* from Petal Templates 4, 5, and 6) Use 6 petals per sunflower.
⅛ yd. medium gold print (or use scraps)	9 petals* (3 *each* from Petal Templates 4, 5, and 6) Use 3 petals per sunflower.
⅝ yd. fabric for backing	
21" x 37" rectangle of batting	
1 skein *each* of rust and black embroidery thread (or use quilting thread)	
12 orange buttons in assorted sizes	
17 brown buttons in assorted sizes	

* Cut leaves and petals, using the templates on pages 52–53, as directed for the appliqué method you prefer. (See the appliqué sections in "General Instructions" on pages 8–9.) The quilt in the photo was appliquéd using the cheater method.

** For Leaf Templates 1 and 2, reverse the template and cut 1. For Leaf Template 3, reverse the template and cut 2.

Directions

1. Following the instructions on page 12 for measuring and adding borders, cut the 1¼"-wide striped top and bottom border strips and sew them to the 11½" x 29" blue rectangle, then add the side border strips. Press seam allowances away from the quilt center.

2. Measure and cut the 3½"-wide blue top and bottom border strips and sew them to the quilt top; repeat for the side border strips. Press seam allowances away from the quilt center.

3. Referring to the diagram below for leaf placement, position leaves for each flower cut from Templates 1, 2, and 3.

Note

The upper and lower flowers each have 3 leaves; the middle flower has 2 leaves.

4. Place each flower center so that it slightly overlaps the top of the leaves. *Pin in place only; do not appliqué.* Start with the bottom flower first. Position the top flower next, then the middle flower. (You will need to position the petals so they will be covered by the center.) If you are using hand appliqué, make sure you position the ends of the petals under the flower center's *seam line.* Remove the center each time you position a layer of petals, then replace it for the next layer.

5. Referring to the diagram for petal layout, position the dark petals cut from Petal Templates 4, 5, and 6. Place the colors randomly. Tuck the ends of all petals under the edge of the flower center.

6. Position the medium-color petals cut from Petal Templates 4, 5, and 6, arranging these lighter petals to cover background area between the darker bottom petals.

7. Position the small petals cut from Petal Templates 7 and 8. Arrange these petals to form a ring around the center, barely touching or overlapping each other.

Before appliquéing or fusing, adjust all petals to cover all background showing through the flowers. Take your time to shape all 3 flowers to your preference.

8. Appliqué all flower pieces, choosing one of the methods described in the box on the following page.

Cheater Appliqué

When all the pieces are arranged, pin, then baste securely. Baste around the flower center first to catch the ends of the petals, quickly eliminating many of the pins, making appliqué easier.

Use a single strand of embroidery floss or quilting thread; use black for the leaves, and rust for the petals and centers.

Hand Appliqué

Once the pieces for all three flowers are positioned, pin in place. Use a fabric marking pen or pencil to lightly mark a dot where the point of each petal in the uppermost layer should be.

Next, remove the center and only those petals that are in the way of hand appliquéing the lower layers.

Hand appliqué the lowest layer. Reposition the next layers, matching the petal points to the dots. Some adjusting may be necessary. Add another petal if needed to fill in gaps.

Trim away excess overlapped petals to reduce bulk if needed. Position and appliqué the flower centers.

Fusible Appliqué

Once the pieces for all three flowers are positioned, fuse according to the manufacturer's instructions. Be sure to remove any pins before applying heat.

If desired, add top stitching or a buttonhole stitch around the edges of the leaves, centers, and a few of the petals.

For more information on these appliqué methods, see pages 8–9.

9. Layer the completed quilt top with batting and backing; baste.

10. Hand or machine quilt in-the-ditch around the borders, or use a pattern of your choice.
11. Bind the edges.
12. Sew the buttons to the quilt in a random pattern. Refer to the quilt plan on page 48.
13. Add a hanging sleeve. (See page 16.)

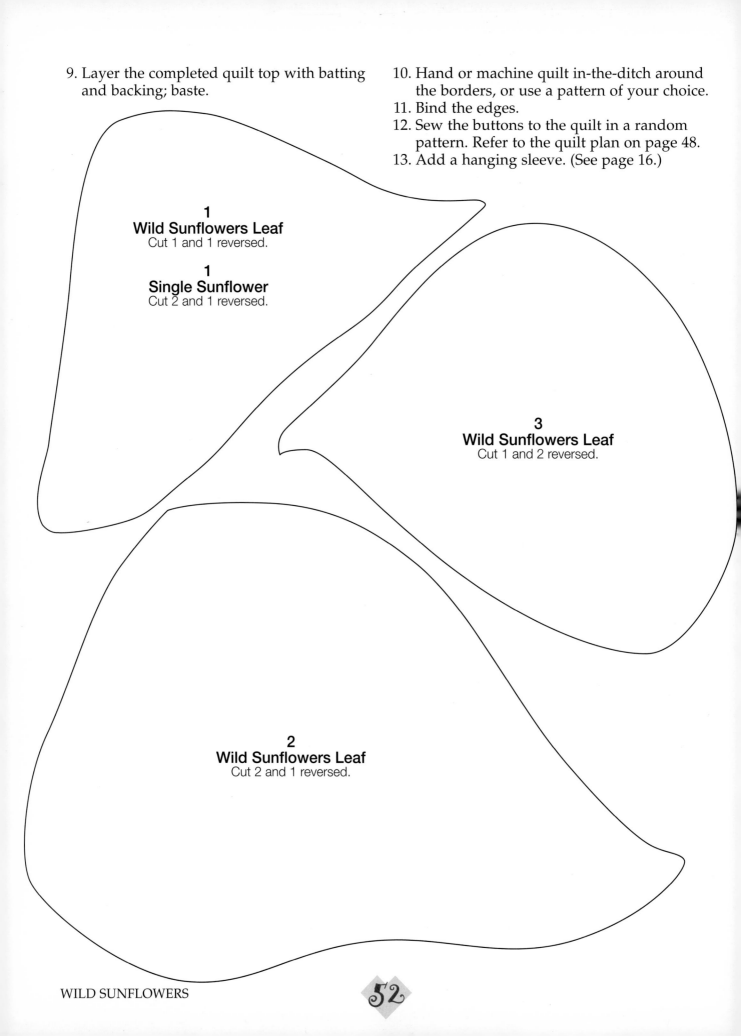

1
Wild Sunflowers Leaf
Cut 1 and 1 reversed.

1
Single Sunflower
Cut 2 and 1 reversed.

3
Wild Sunflowers Leaf
Cut 1 and 2 reversed.

2
Wild Sunflowers Leaf
Cut 2 and 1 reversed.

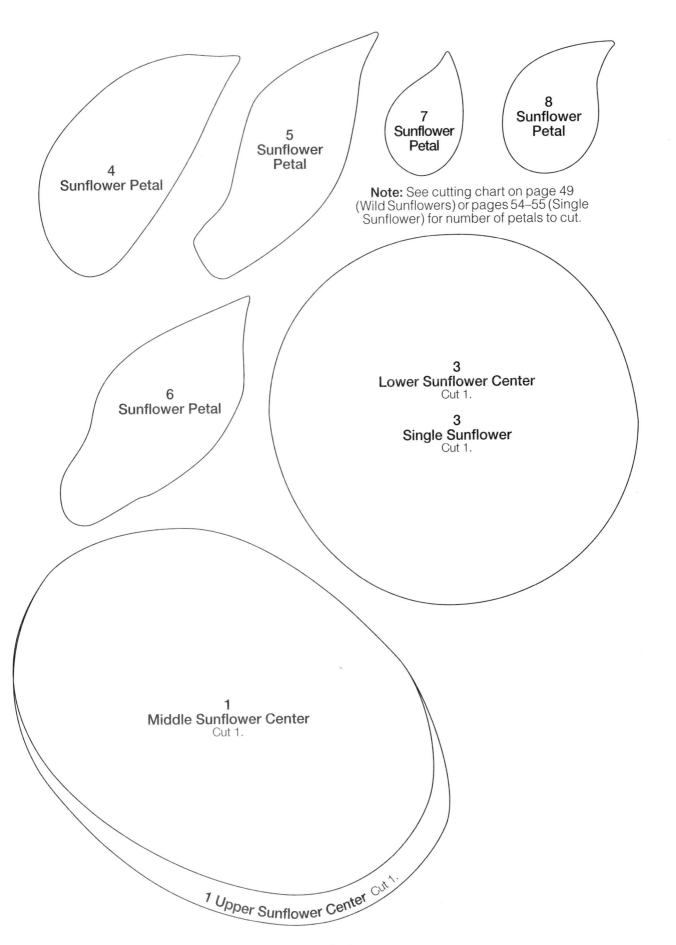

4
Sunflower Petal

5
Sunflower
Petal

7
Sunflower
Petal

8
Sunflower
Petal

Note: See cutting chart on page 49 (Wild Sunflowers) or pages 54–55 (Single Sunflower) for number of petals to cut.

6
Sunflower Petal

3
Lower Sunflower Center
Cut 1.

3
Single Sunflower
Cut 1.

1
Middle Sunflower Center
Cut 1.

1 Upper Sunflower Center Cut 1.

Single Sunflower

Finished Size: 17" x 17"
Color Photo: Page 22
Templates: Pages 52–53

MATERIALS	CUTTING
½ yd. muslin for background and border	1 square, 9" x 9"
	2 strips, each 3½" x 42"
⅛ yd. striped print for inner border and binding	1 strip, 1½" x 42"
	2 strips, each 1¼" x 42"
⅛ yd. green print	3 leaves (Leaf Template 1)**
⅛ yd. black print (or use scraps)	1 flower center* (Lower Flower Center Template)
⅛ yd. dark orange solid (or use scraps)	5 petals* (combined from Petal Templates 4, 5, and 6)
⅛ yd. dark gold solid (or use scraps)	4 petals* (combined from Petal Templates 4, 5, and 6)
⅛ yd. light yellow solid (or use scraps)	13 petals* (combined from Petal Templates 7 and 8)
⅛ yd. medium gold solid (or use scraps)	6 petals* (2 *each* from Petal Templates 4, 5, and 6)

MATERIALS	CUTTING
⅛ yd. light yellow print (or use scraps)	6 petals* (2 *each* from Petal Template 4, 5, and 6)
⅛ yd. medium gold print (or use scraps)	2 petals* (1 *each* from Petal Templates 5 and 6)
⅝ yd. fabric for backing	
19" x 19" square of batting	
1 skein each of rust and black embroidery floss (for cheater appliqué)	
13 assorted small orange buttons	

* Cut leaves, petals, and centers, using the templates on pages 52–53, as directed for the appliqué method you prefer. (See the appliqué sections in "General Instructions" on pages 8–9.) The quilt in the photo was appliquéd using the cheater method.

** Reverse the template and cut one leaf.

NOTE: For a more varied appearance, cut the petals using both sides of the template or cut some petals freehand. Speed up the cutting process by cutting fabric in layers.

Directions

1. Following the instructions on page 12 for measuring and adding borders, cut the 1½"-wide striped top and bottom border strips and sew them to the 9" square, then add the side border strips. Press the seam allowances away from the quilt center.
2. Measure and cut the 3½"-wide muslin top and bottom border strips and sew them to the quilt top; repeat for the side border strips. Press the seam allowances away from the quilt center.
3. For leaf, petal, and flower center placement, follow the directions for making sunflowers in steps 3–8 for the Wild Sunflowers quilt on page 50 using only Leaf Template 1 for leaves. See diagram at right for leaf placement. Appliqué, using the method of your choice. (See page 51.) If you use the cheater method, stitch the leaves with a single strand of black embroidery floss; use rust floss for the petals and center.
4. Layer the completed quilt top with batting and backing; baste.
5. Hand or machine quilt in-the-ditch around the borders, or quilt as desired.
6. Bind the edges.
7. Sew orange buttons in a random pattern to the outer border.
8. Add a hanging sleeve. (See page 16.)

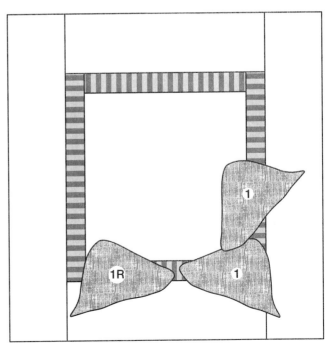

Basic Botania

Finished Size: 17½" x 23"
Color Photo: Page 23
Templates: Page 58

MATERIALS	CUTTING
¼ yd. red-on-red print for background	6 squares, each 6" x 6"
¼ yd. white-on-white print for flowers and border	6 flowers*
	2 strips, each 1¼" x 42"
⅓ yd. green-on-green print for centers, stems, border, and binding	6 flower centers*
	4 bias strips, each ¼" x 5"
	2 strips, each 1" x 42"
	2 strips, each 1¼" x 42"
	2 strips, each 2½" x 42"
¼ yd. red-and-white check for border	
⅝ yd. fabric for backing	
20" x 25" rectangle of batting	
1¾ yds. of ⅜"-wide green ribbon	

MATERIALS	CUTTING
1 skein each of gold and green embroidery floss	
6 medium-size purple buttons	
4 large red buttons	

* Cut flowers and centers, using the templates on page 58, as directed for the appliqué method you prefer. (See the appliqué sections in "General Instructions" on pages 8–9.) When cutting, reverse the templates occasionally for a random, more natural look. The quilt in the photo was appliquéd using the cheater method.

Directions

1. Sew the 6 red-on-red print squares together as shown and press seams in opposite directions from row to row.

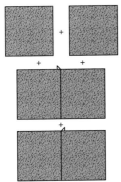

2. Pin a prepared white-on-white print flower to the center of each 6" red-on-red print square, leaving a ¼"-wide seam allowance on the outside edges of the blocks.

3. Position and pin the stems so that they cross at the intersection of the red-on-red squares as shown. (For a not-so-perfect look, cut the stems freehand.) Tuck the stem ends under the white flowers, trimming if they show through the flower fabric.

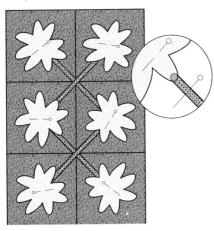

4. Pin a green flower center to each flower in the position of your choice.

5. Appliqué or fuse the flowers, centers, and stems, using the appliqué method you prefer. For cheater appliqué, outline with a running stitch, using 2 strands of gold embroidery floss.

6. Following the instructions on page 12 for measuring and adding borders, cut the 1¼"-wide white-on-white top and bottom border strips and sew them to the quilt top, then add the side border strips. Press seam allowances away from the quilt center.

7. Measure and cut the 1"-wide green-on-green top and bottom border strips and sew them to the quilt top; repeat for the side border strips.

8. Measure and cut the 2½"-wide red-and-white checked top and bottom border strips and sew them to the quilt top; repeat for the side border strips. Press seam allowances away from the quilt center.

BASIC BOTANIA

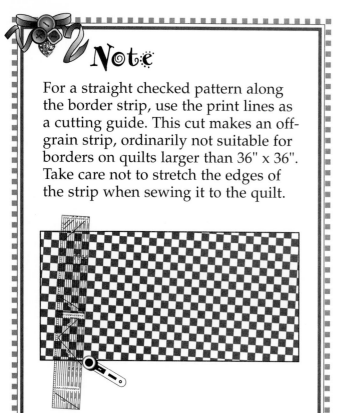

12. Embellish with a single purple button and a green ribbon bow on each flower center.

13. Sew a large red button to each corner of the ½"-wide green border, using green embroidery floss.
14. Add a hanging sleeve. (See page 16.)

9. Layer the completed quilt top with batting and backing; baste.
10. Hand or machine quilt, or tie as desired.
11. Bind the edges.

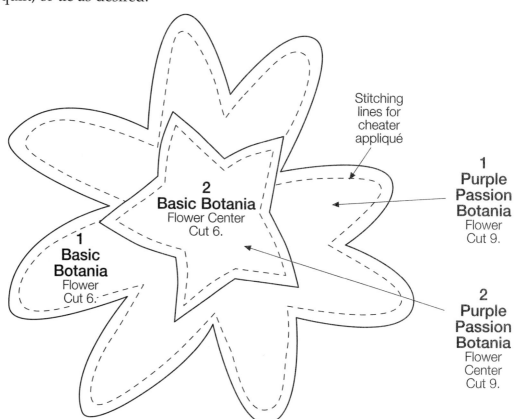

Stitching lines for cheater appliqué

1 Purple Passion Botania Flower Cut 9.

2 Purple Passion Botania Flower Center Cut 9.

2 Basic Botania Flower Center Cut 6.

1 Basic Botania Flower Cut 6.

Purple Passion Botania

Finished Size: 24½" x 24½"
Color Photo: Page 24
Templates: Pages 58, 61

MATERIALS	CUTTING
⅜ yd. white-on-white print for background	9 squares, each 6" x 6"
⅜ yd. medium purple print for flowers, border, and binding	6 flowers*
	4 strips, each 1¼" x 42"
3 squares, each 5" x 5", of dark purple prints for flowers (or use scraps)	3 flowers*
Assorted scraps of medium green print for flower centers	3 centers*
Assorted scraps of dark green print for flower centers	6 centers*
½ yd. black-and-dark-purple print for borders	3 strips, 3½" x 42"

* Cut 9 flowers and 9 centers, using the templates from Basic Botania on page 58, as directed for the appliqué method you prefer. (See the appliqué sections in "General Instructions" on pages 8–9.) When cutting, reverse the templates occasionally for a random, more natural look. The quilt in the photo was appliquéd using the cheater method.

Continued on page 60.

Continued from page 59.

MATERIALS	CUTTING
⅞ yd. fabric for backing	
26" x 26" square of batting	
10"-long piece of 4"-wide lace	
2½ yds. of ¼"-wide purple ribbon	
31 assorted small purple, blue, black, and green buttons	
4 large purple buttons	
9 brass bee charms (optional)	
1 skein purple embroidery floss (for cheater appliqué)	
28" of ⅜"-wide green satin ribbon	

Directions

1. Appliqué or fuse each flower to the center of a 6" white-on-white print square, using the appliqué method you prefer. For cheater appliqué, outline with a running stitch, using 2 strands of purple embroidery floss.

 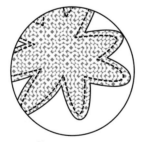

Cheater appliqué

> ### Note
> If using the fusible method, layer flower centers and flowers on muslin and fuse at the same time.

2. Appliqué or fuse a medium green center to each dark purple flower, and a dark green center to each medium purple flower.

3. Arrange the 9 blocks together in rows of 3 as shown. Sew the blocks into rows. Press seam allowances in opposite directions from row to row.

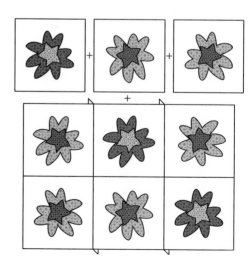

4. Following the instructions on page 12 for measuring and adding borders, cut the 1¼"-wide medium purple top and bottom border strips and sew them to the quilt top, then add the side border strips. Press seam allowances away from the quilt center.

5. Measure and cut the 3½"-wide black-and-dark-purple border strips and sew them to the top and bottom of the quilt top; repeat for the side border strips.

6. Layer the completed quilt top with batting and backing; baste.

7. Hand or machine quilt before adding button embellishments. Follow the suggested quilt pattern, below right, or use a pattern of your choice.

8. Bind the edges.

9. Embellish each flower's center with a purple bow and 3 buttons. (I couldn't resist adding a little bee charm to each flower!) Sew a button to each block intersection, in the center of each quilted flower, as shown in the diagram.

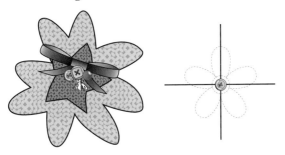

10. Cut across the 10" piece of lace to make 4 pieces, each measuring 2½" long. Gather along the center of each piece as shown.

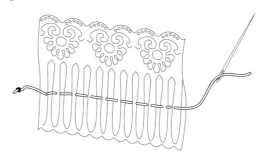

11. Loop a 7"-long piece of green ribbon and pin, crossing the lace segment, at each corner of the medium purple border. Refer to the quilt plan on page 59 for placement. Secure with a large purple button.

12. Add a hanging sleeve. (See page 16.)

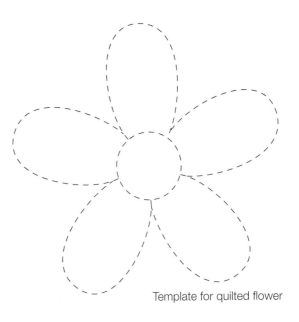

Template for quilted flower

Potted Whimsy

Finished Size: 31" x 31"
Color Photo: Page 25

MATERIALS	CUTTING
1¼ yds. gold print or solid for background and borders	12 squares, each 3" x 3"
	6 rectangles, each 4" x 8"
	4 strips, each 1½" x 7"
	2 strips, each 1½" x 3¼"
	1 rectangle, 4¼" x 8"
	6 strips, each 1" x 15"
	2 strips, each 1¼" x 23"
	2 strips, each 1¼" x 24½"
	12 strips, each 1½" x 26"
⅓ yd. green stripe for stems, inner border, and binding	3 strips, each 1" x 8"*
	2 strips, each 1" x 24½"
	2 strips, each 1" x 25½"
	3 strips, each 1¼" x 42"
⅓ yd. dark rust print or solid for pots and border	2 rectangles, each 6" x 7"
	1 rectangle, 3¼" x 6"
	2 strips, each 1½" x 26"
⅛ yd. medium rust for pot rims	3 strips, each 1½" x 8"
⅓ yd. red print or solid for flower and border	3 strips, each 1" x 15"
	4 strips, each 1½" x 26"

■ *Cut one 1" x 8" green stripe stem across the fabric width, cut the other 2 lengthwise.

MATERIALS	CUTTING
⅓ yd. purple print or solid for flower and border	3 strips, each 1" x 15"
	4 strips, each 1½" x 26"
⅓ yd. orange print or solid for flower and border	3 strips, each 1" x 15"
	2 strips, each 1½" x 26"
⅛ yd. black print for flower centers	3 squares, each 3" x 3"
1½ yds. of ⅝"-wide green ribbon	
1 yd. of ⅛"-wide green ribbon	
3 medium-size black buttons	
7 large red, purple, and orange buttons	
6 medium-size green buttons	
12 *each* of small red, purple, and orange buttons	
27 small brown buttons	
19 brass charms (optional)	

Directions

BLOCKS

1. Sew a 4" x 8" rectangle of gold background fabric to each side of a 1" x 8" green stem strip. Press the seam allowances toward stem strip.

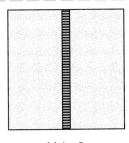

Make 3.

2. For each large pot, sew a 1½" x 7" gold background strip to each side of a 6" x 7" dark rust rectangle as shown. For the small pot, sew a 1½" x 3¼" gold background strip to each side of a 3¼" x 6" dark rust rectangle as shown. Press seam allowances toward the pot.

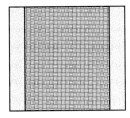 

Make 2.   Make 1.

3. Sew a 1½" x 8" medium rust strip across the top of each pot block as shown. Press seam allowances toward the strip.

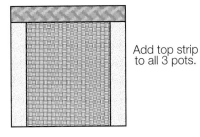

Add top strip to all 3 pots.

4. Sew a stem block to the top of each pot block as shown. Press seam allowances toward the pot.

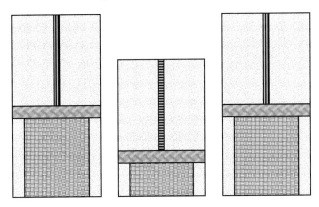

5. Using 1" x 15" strips, make 1 strip-pieced unit for each color flower, alternating 2 strips of gold background with 3 strips of the same flower color as shown. Press seam allowances in one direction.

3"

¾"
½"
½"
½"
¾"

Note

Be sure to sew accurate ¼"-wide seams. The strip-pieced unit should measure 3" wide, with each inner strip's width exactly ½".

6. Cut across each strip-pieced unit at 3" intervals to make 4 squares of each flower color.

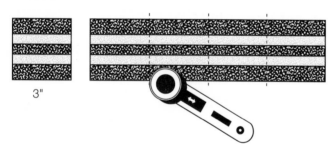

3"

7. Assemble Ninepatch flower blocks as shown, combining the 4 strip-pieced units with a 3" black print square for each flower center, and a 3" gold square in each corner. Press seams in opposite directions from row to row.

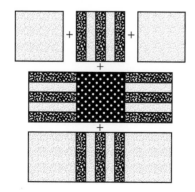

8. Sew a 4¼" x 8" gold background rectangle to the top of the center (purple) flower *only* as shown. Press seam allowances toward the background rectangle.

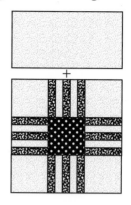

9. Sew the red and orange flower blocks to each large pot and stem unit. Sew the purple flower block to the small pot and stem unit. Press seam allowances toward the stems.

10. Sew the 3 potted flower units together, placing the purple-flowered, small pot unit at the center as shown. Press seam allowances away from the center.

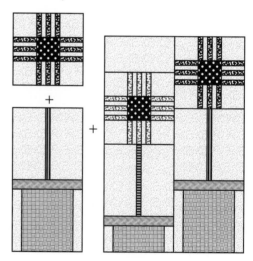

BORDERS

1. Sew the 1¼" x 23" gold top and bottom border strips to the quilt top, then add the 1¼" x 24½" side border strips. Press the seam allowances away from the quilt center.
2. Sew the 1" x 24½" green stripe border strips to the top and bottom of the quilt, then repeat for the 1" x 25½" side border strips. Press the seam allowances away from the quilt center.

3. To make Strip-Pieced Unit 1, alternate a 1½" x 26" gold strip with a 1½" x 26" strip each of dark rust, purple, and red in the order shown below. Press seam allowances toward the outer gold strip. Make 2 strip-pieced units.

Note

Be sure to sew accurate ¼"-wide seams. The strip-pieced unit should measure exactly 6½" wide, with each inner strip measuring 1" wide.

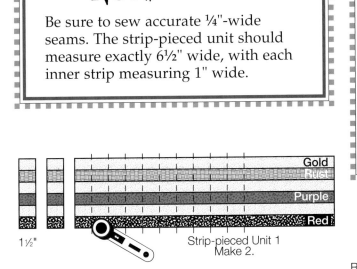

Strip-pieced Unit 1
Make 2.

1½"

4. To make Strip-Pieced Unit 2, alternate a 1½" x 26" gold strip with a 1½" x 26" strip each of orange, purple, and red in the order shown below. Press seam allowances toward the outer gold strip. Make 2 strip-pieced units.

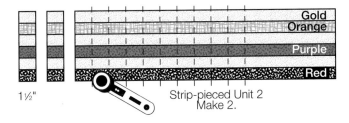

Strip-pieced Unit 2
Make 2.

1½"

5. Referring to the diagrams above, cut across one strip-pieced Unit 1, and one strip-pieced Unit 2 at 1½" intervals. Cut 12 segments from each. Keep Unit 1 segments separate from Unit 2 segments.

6. For each row of the strip-pieced border, join 4 rectangles end to end, alternating rectangles cut from Units 1 and 2 in the order shown above right. Begin Row 1 with a

Unit 1 rectangle and begin Row 2 with a Unit 2 rectangle, paying attention to color placement as shown.

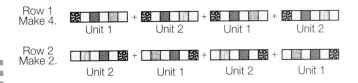

Row 1 Make 4.
Unit 1   Unit 2   Unit 1   Unit 2

Row 2 Make 2.
Unit 2   Unit 1   Unit 2   Unit 1

Note

Measure the rows. If the measurement is different than the measurement of the quilt top, resew a few of the squares, taking a *slightly* deeper or shallower seam allowance until the row is the right length.

7. Sew a Row 1 to each side of a Row 2 to make top border as shown.

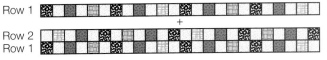

Row 1
Row 2
Row 1

8. Cut another 1½"-wide segment from Unit 1 or Unit 2 and remove 3 squares. Add to one end of the top border as shown in the diagram below.

1½"

9. Repeat steps 7 and 8 for bottom border. Stitch top and bottom borders to quilt top.

10. For the side borders, repeat steps 5–7, cutting 14 segments from the remaining Unit 1, and 16 segments from the remaining Unit 2. Join 5 rectangles end to end for each row, paying attention to color placement as shown below, left. Cut and add a partial rectangle to one end of each row as shown in the diagram below, right. Sew side borders to quilt top.

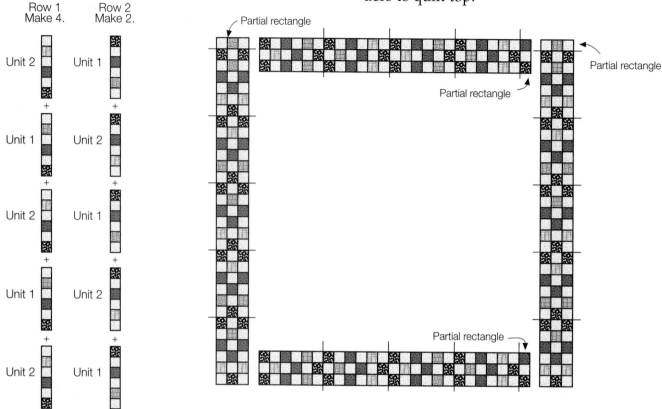

Row 1
Make 4.

Row 2
Make 2.

Unit 2 + Unit 1 + Unit 2 + Unit 1 + Unit 2

Unit 1 + Unit 2 + Unit 1 + Unit 2 + Unit 1

Partial rectangle

Partial rectangle

Partial rectangle

Partial rectangle

FINISHING THE QUILT

1. Layer the completed quilt top with batting and backing; baste.
2. Hand or machine quilt in-the-ditch or use a quilt pattern of your choice. The background in the quilt pictured on page 25 was stipple-quilted by machine. Rows of stipple quilting stitches lie close together, approximately ⅛"–¼" apart. The rows of stitches are randomly placed so that no overall pattern is established.

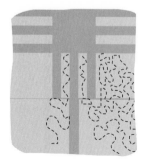

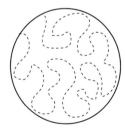

3. Bind the edges.

4. Use a ⅝"-wide green ribbon bow for the leaves. Twist the ribbon ends and tack with a matching thread, hiding knots under the ribbon. Sew a green button to each ribbon end. Sew a black button to each ribbon "knot" as shown.

5. Sew a button to each petal end, matching colors if desired. Sew a large button to the flower center.
6. Sew a row of brown buttons just under the rim on the center pot, and another across the bottom of each outer pot.
7. Sew a large button to each corner of the green striped border. (I secured each button with a ⅛"-wide green ribbon.)
8. Sew brass charms randomly to the pieced border if desired.
9. Add a hanging sleeve. (See page 16.)

One Whimsy

Finished size: 15" x 29½"
Color Photo: Page 26

MATERIALS	CUTTING
⅝ yd. purple print or solid for background and borders	4 squares, each 3" x 3"
	2 rectangles, each 4" x 8"
	2 rectangles, each 1½" x 7"
	2 strips, each 1" x 15"
	2 strips, each 1¼" x 42"
	3 strips, each 2½" x 42
¼ yd. gold print for flower and binding	3 strips, each 1" x 15"
	3 strips, each 1¼" x 42"
⅛ yd. green stripe for stem and inner border*	1 strip, 1" x 8"
	2 strips, each 1" x 42"

* If you want to cut the 1" x 8" stem strip on the lengthwise grain, increase yardage to ¼ yard.

Continued on page 68.

Continued from page 67.

MATERIALS	CUTTING
¼ yd. orange print for flower center and inner border	1 square, 3" x 3"
	2 strips, each 1" x 42"
⅛ yd. medium rust for pot rim	1 strip, 1½" x 8"
¼ yd. dark rust for pot	1 rectangle, 6" x 7"
½ yd. fabric for backing	
17" x 32" rectangle of batting	
18" of ⅜"-wide green grosgrain ribbon	
15 medium-size black beads	
12 small orange buttons	
1 medium-size red button	
2 small and 4 large black buttons	
9 small brown buttons	

Directions

1. Assemble 1 each of the flower, stem, and flowerpot blocks, following steps 1–9 for a large flower pot unit in the Potted Whimsy quilt on pages 63–64 and substituting colors as needed.

2. Following the instructions on page 12 for measuring and adding borders, cut the 1¼"-wide purple border strips and sew them to the top and bottom of the quilt top, then add the side border strips. Press the seam allowances away from the quilt center.

3. Measure and cut the 1"-wide green stripe border strips and sew them to the top and bottom of the quilt top; repeat for the side border strips.

4. Measure and cut the 1"-wide orange print border strips and sew them to the top and bottom of the quilt top; repeat for the side border strips.

5. Measure and cut the 2½"-wide purple border strips and sew them to the top and bottom of the quilt top; repeat for the side border strips.

6. Layer the completed quilt top with batting and backing; baste.

7. Hand or machine quilt in-the-ditch or use a quilt pattern of your choice.

8. Bind the edges.

9. Use a ⅜"-wide green ribbon bow for the leaves. Twist the ribbon ends and tack with a matching thread, hiding knots under the ribbon. Sew a small black button to each ribbon end; sew a red button to make the ribbon "knot."

10. Sew an orange button to each petal end. Sew black beads to the flower center.

11. Sew a row of brown buttons to the pot in the shape of a pyramid as shown in the photo on page 67.

12. Sew a large black button to each corner of the green striped border.

13. Add a hanging sleeve. (See page 16.)

Potted Heartsies

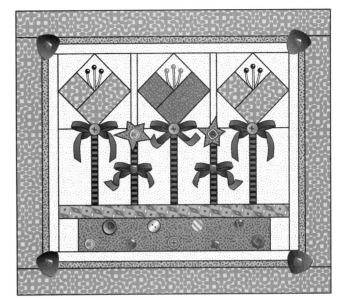

Finished Size: 25¹/₂" x 21"
Color Photo: Page 27
Templates: Page 72

MATERIALS	CUTTING
½ yd. gold print or solid for background and inner border	3 squares, each 2½" x 2½"
	6 squares, each 3¾" x 3¾"
	6 rectangles, each 3⅛" x 6¼"
	2 rectangles, each 2" x 3"
	2 strips, each 1" x 7"
	2 strips, each 1¼" x 42"
⅛ yd. green stripe for stems	3 strips, each 1" x 6¼"
	2 strips, each 1" x 5"
⅛ yd. medium rust for rim	1 strip, 1½" x 18¾"
⅛ yd. dark rust for pot	1 rectangle, 3" x 15¾"
½ yd. purple for 2 flowers, outer border, and binding	2 squares, each 2½" x 2½"
	2 rectangles, each 2½" x 4½"
	3 strips, each 2½" x 42"
	3 strips, each 1¼" x 42"
¼ yd. red for flowers and middle border	1 square, 2½" x 2½"
	1 rectangle, 2½" x 4½"
	2 stars*
	2 strips, each 1" x 42"

* Cut stars, using the templates on page 72, as directed for the appliqué method you prefer. (See the appliqué sections in "General Instructions" on pages 8–9.) The quilt in the photo was appliquéd using the fusible method.

Continued on page 70.

Continued from page 69.

MATERIALS	CUTTING
⅞ yd. fabric for backing	
23" x 28" rectangle of batting	
20" *each* of ⅜"-wide purple and green grosgrain ribbon	
10" of ⅜"-wide red ribbon	
9 large glass beads in assorted coordinating colors	
6 small and 3 medium-size red buttons	
9 brown buttons in assorted sizes	
4 large and 2 medium-size black buttons	

Directions

1. Sew a 3⅛" x 6¼" gold rectangle to each side of a 1" x 6¼" green stem strip. Press seam allowances toward stem strip.

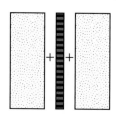

2. Sew a 2½" gold square to each 2½" purple or red square of flower fabric. Press seam allowances toward the flower square.

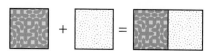

3. Sew a 2½" x 4½" red or purple rectangle to the flower unit as shown, matching flower colors. Press toward the flower rectangle.

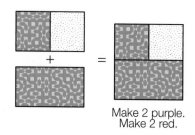

Make 2 purple.
Make 2 red.

4. Cut each 3¾" background square once diagonally to make a total of 12 triangles.

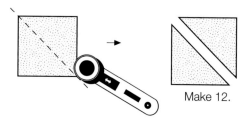

Make 12.

5. Sew a triangle along its long side to opposite corners of each flower unit as shown. Press seam allowances toward the triangles. Sew a triangle to each remaining corner; press.

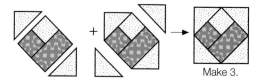

Make 3.

PIECING HINT: With right sides together, align the point of the triangle at the center of the square. For a smooth block edge, begin and end stitching at the **V** as shown below.

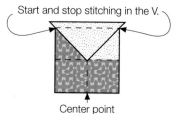

Start and stop stitching in the V.

Center point

POTTED HEARTSIES

6. Sew a flower block to each stem block. Press seam allowances toward stem block.

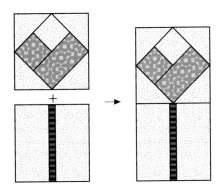

7. Sew a 1" x 5" green stripe strip to each 1" x 7" background strip, end to end.

8. Alternate flower units with stem units as shown. Stitch and press seam allowances under the stem unit.

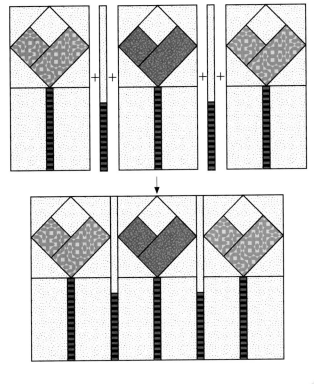

9. Sew a 1½" x 18¾" medium rust strip across the bottom of the stems as shown. Press seam allowances toward strip.

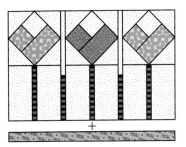

10. Sew a 2" x 3" background rectangle to each end of the 3" x 15¾" dark rust rectangle as shown. Press seam allowances toward the flower pot.

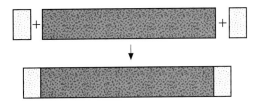

11. Stitch flower pot to rim. Press seam allowances toward the rim.

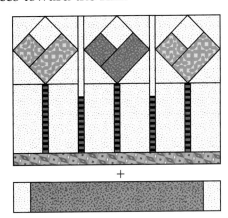

12. Following the instructions on page 12 for measuring and adding borders, cut the 1¼"-wide gold side border strips and sew them to the quilt top, then add the top and bottom border strips. Press the seam allowances away from the quilt center.
13. Measure and cut the 1"-wide red border strips and sew them to the sides of the quilt top; repeat for the top and bottom border strips.
14. Measure and cut the 2½"-wide purple border strips and sew them to the sides of the quilt top; repeat for the top and bottom border strips.

POTTED HEARTSIES

15. Using the templates below, prepare red star flowers according to the appliqué method you prefer. Appliqué a star flower to the end of each short stem as shown. Using embroidery floss or quilting thread, make a line of running stitches ⅛" inside the flower's edge.

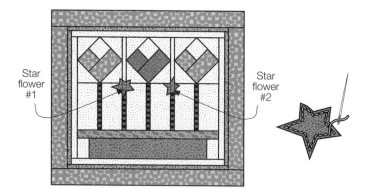

Star flower #1

Star flower #2

FINISHING TOUCHES

1. Embroider 3 stems from the **V** of each pieced flower and attach a button or glass bead at the outer ends as shown.

2. Layer the completed quilt top with batting and backing; baste.
3. Hand or machine quilt in-the-ditch or use a quilt pattern of your choice.
4. Bind the edges.
5. Use a ⅜"-wide green ribbon bow for the "leaves" on the two star-flower stems. Twist the ribbon ends and tack with a matching thread, hiding knots under the ribbon. Sew a small red button to make the ribbon "knot."
6. Use a ⅜"-wide red or purple ribbon bow at the base of each pieced flower, matching flower colors. Tack the ribbon as above and sew a medium-size red button to make the ribbon "knot."

7. Sew a medium-size black button to the center of each red star flower.
8. Sew 9 brown buttons in a zigzag row across the flower pot.
9. Sew a large black button to each corner of the red middle border. Sew a small red button on top of each large black button as shown.

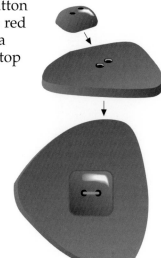

10. Add a hanging sleeve. (See page 16.)

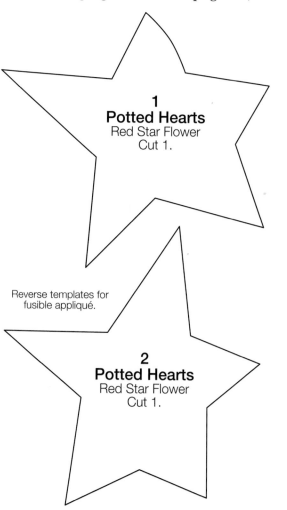

1
Potted Hearts
Red Star Flower
Cut 1.

Reverse templates for fusible appliqué.

2
Potted Hearts
Red Star Flower
Cut 1.

Single Heartsy

Finished Size: 13¼" x 21¼"
Color Photo: Page 28

MATERIALS	CUTTING
¼ yd. gold print or solid for background	1 square, 2½" x 2½"
	2 squares, 3¾" x 3¾"
	2 rectangles, 3⅛" x 4½"
	2 rectangles, 1¼" x 3"
	1 strip, 1¼" x 42"
⅛ yd. green stripe for stems	1 strip, 1" x 4½"
	1 strip, 1" x 6¼"
⅛ yd. orange for flowers and inner border	1 square, 2½" x 2½"
	1 rectangle, 2½" x 4½"
	2 strips, ¾" x 42"
⅛ yd. medium rust for pot rim	1 rectangle, 1½" x 6¼"
⅛ yd. dark rust for pot	1 rectangle, 3" x 4¾"

Continued on page 74.

Continued from page 73.

MATERIALS	CUTTING
¼ yd. black for inner border and binding	2 strips, 1" x 42"
	2 strips, 1¼" x 42"
¼ yd. green check or print for outer border	2 strips, 2½" x 42"
½ yd. fabric for backing	
15" x 23" rectangle of batting	
18" of ⅜"-wide green grosgrain ribbon	
3 large black beads	
4 small, 1 medium-size, and 4 large black buttons	
5 small brown buttons	
4 small orange buttons	

Directions

1. Make the pieced flower, following steps 2–5 of the directions on page 70 for Potted Heartsies. (When you cut the 3¾" x 3¾" background squares, you'll get 4 triangles.)

2. Sew a 3⅛" x 4½" gold background rectangle to each side of a 1" x 4½" green stem strip as shown. Press seam allowances toward the stem strip.

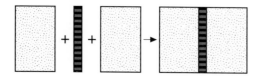

3. Sew a 1" x 6¼" horizontal green strip to the top of the stem block as shown. Press seam allowances toward horizontal green strip.

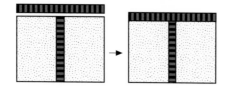

4. Sew the stem block to the flower block as shown. Press the seam allowances toward the horizontal green strip.

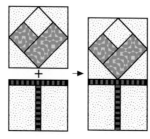

5. Sew a 1½" x 6¼" medium rust rectangle to the bottom of the stem block. Press seam allowances toward the rectangle.

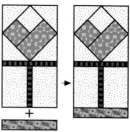

6. Sew a 1¼" x 3" gold background rectangle to each side of the 3" x 4¾" dark rust flower pot rectangle. Press seam allowances toward the pot.

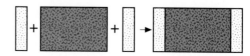

7. Sew the pot unit to the rim as shown. Press seam allowances toward the rim.

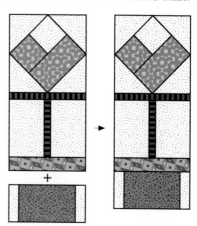

8. Following the instructions on page 12 for measuring and adding borders, cut the 1¼"-wide gold top and bottom border strips and sew them to the quilt top, then add the side border strips. Press the seam allowances away from the quilt center.

9. Measure and cut the 1"-wide black border strips and sew them to the top and bottom of the quilt top; repeat for the side border strips.

10. Measure and cut the ¾"-wide orange border strips and sew them to the top and bottom of the quilt top; repeat for the side border strips.

11. Measure and cut the 2½"-wide green check border strips and sew them to the sides of the quilt top; repeat for the top and bottom border strips.

FINISHING TOUCHES

1. Embroider 3 stems from the V of each pieced flower and attach a button or glass bead at the outer ends as shown.

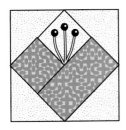

2. Layer the completed quilt top with batting and backing; baste.
3. Hand or machine quilt in-the-ditch or use a quilt pattern of your choice.

4. Bind the edges.
5. Use a ⅜"-wide green ribbon bow for the "leaves." Twist the ribbon ends and tack with a matching thread, hiding knots under the ribbon. Sew a medium-size black button to make the ribbon "knot," and sew a small black button to each ribbon end. Sew a small black button to each end of the horizontal green strip.

6. Sew 5 small brown buttons across pot rim.
7. Sew a large black button to each corner of the ¾"-wide orange border. Sew a small orange button on top of each large black button as shown on page 72.
8. Add a hanging sleeve. (See page 16.)

Resources

Buttons and brass charms as suggested embellishments in this book can be ordered from:

By Jupiter!®
6801 North 21st Avenue
Suite "O"
Phoenix, AZ 85015
1-800-242-2574

That Patchwork Place Publications and Products

BOOKS

All the Blocks Are Geese by Mary Sue Suit
Angle Antics by Mary Hickey
Animas Quilts by Jackie Robinson
Appliqué Borders: An Added Grace by Jeana Kimball
Appliquilt: Whimsical One-Step Appliqué by Tonee White
Baltimore Bouquets by Mimi Dietrich
Basket Garden by Mary Hickey
Biblical Blocks by Rosemary Makhan
Blockbuster Quilts by Margaret J. Miller
Botanical Wreaths by Laura M. Reinstatler
Calendar Quilts by Joan Hanson
Cathedral Window: A Fresh Look by Nancy J. Martin
The Cat's Meow by Janet Kime
Colourwash Quilts by Deirdre Amsden
Corners in the Cabin by Paulette Peters
Country Medallion Sampler by Carol Doak
Country Threads by Connie Tesene and Mary Tendall
Easy Machine Paper Piecing by Carol Doak
Easy Quilts...By Jupiter!® by Mary Beth Maison
Even More by Trudie Hughes
Fantasy Flowers by Doreen Cronkite Burbank
Fit To Be Tied by Judy Hopkins
Five- and Seven-Patch Blocks & Quilts for the ScrapSaver by Judy Hopkins
Four-Patch Blocks & Quilts for the ScrapSaver by Judy Hopkins
Fun with Fat Quarters by Nancy J. Martin
Go Wild with Quilts by Margaret Rolfe
Handmade Quilts by Mimi Dietrich
Happy Endings by Mimi Dietrich
Holiday Happenings by Christal Carter
Home for Christmas by Nancy J. Martin and Sharon Stanley
In The Beginning by Sharon Evans Yenter
Irma's Sampler by Irma Eskes
Jacket Jazz by Judy Murrah
Lessons in Machine Piecing by Marsha McCloskey
Little By Little: Quilts in Miniature by Mary Hickey
Little Quilts by Alice Berg, Sylvia Johnson, and Mary Ellen Von Holt
Lively Little Logs by Donna McConnell
Loving Stitches by Jeana Kimball
Make Room for Quilts by Nancy J. Martin
More Template-Free® *Quiltmaking* by Trudie Hughes
Nifty Ninepatches by Carolann M. Palmer
Nine-Patch Blocks & Quilts for the ScrapSaver by Judy Hopkins
Not Just Quilts by Jo Parrott

On to Square Two by Marsha McCloskey
Osage County Quilt Factory by Virginia Robertson
Painless Borders by Sally Schneider
A Perfect Match by Donna Lynn Thomas
Picture Perfect Patchwork by Naomi Norman
Piecemakers® *Country Store* by the Piecemakers
Pineapple Passion by Nancy Smith and Lynda Milligan
A Pioneer Doll and Her Quilts by Mary Hickey
Pioneer Storybook Quilts by Mary Hickey
Prairie People—Cloth Dolls to Make and Cherish by Marji Hadley and J. Dianne Ridgley
Quick & Easy Quiltmaking by Mary Hickey, Nancy J. Martin, Marsha McCloskey and Sara Nephew
Quilted for Christmas compiled by Ursula Reikes
The Quilters' Companion compiled by That Patchwork Place
The Quilting Bee by Jackie Wolff and Lori Aluna
Quilts for All Seasons by Christal Carter
Quilts for Baby: Easy as A, B, C by Ursula Reikes
Quilts for Kids by Carolann M. Palmer
Quilts from Nature by Joan Colvin
Quilts to Share by Janet Kime
Red and Green: An Appliqué Tradition by Jeana Kimball
Red Wagon Originals by Gerry Kimmel and Linda Brannock
Rotary Riot by Judy Hopkins and Nancy J. Martin
Rotary Roundup by Judy Hopkins and Nancy J. Martin
Round About Quilts by J. Michelle Watts
Samplings from the Sea by Rosemary Makhan
Scrap Happy by Sally Schneider
ScrapMania by Sally Schneider
Sensational Settings by Joan Hanson
Sewing on the Line by Lesly-Claire Greenberg
Shortcuts: A Concise Guide to Rotary Cutting by Donna Lynn Thomas (metric version available)
Shortcuts Sampler by Roxanne Carter
Shortcuts to the Top by Donna Lynn Thomas
Small Talk by Donna Lynn Thomas
Smoothstitch™ *Quilts* by Roxi Eppler
The Stitchin' Post by Jean Wells and Lawry Thorn
Strips That Sizzle by Margaret J. Miller
Sunbonnet Sue All Through the Year by Sue Linker
Tea Party Time by Nancy J. Martin
Template-Free® *Quiltmaking* by Trudie Hughes
Template-Free® *Quilts and Borders* by Trudie Hughes
Template-Free® *Stars* by Jo Parrott
Watercolor Quilts by Pat Magaret and Donna Slusser
Women and Their Quilts by Nancyann Johanson Twelker

TOOLS

6" Bias Square®
8" Bias Square®
Metric Bias Square®

BiRangle™
Pineapple Rule
Rotary Mate™

Rotary Rule™
Ruby Beholder™
ScrapMaster

VIDEO

Shortcuts to America's Best-Loved Quilts

Many titles are available at your local quilt shop. For more information, send $2 for a color catalog to That Patchwork Place, Inc., PO Box 118, Bothell WA 98041-0118 USA.

☎ Call 1-800-426-3126 for the name and location of the quilt shop nearest you.